Christianity:

Success or Failure

?

Gustav Shakefoot

ISBN: 1-933899-29-8

Published by:
Holy Fire Publishing
531 Constitution Blvd., Martinsburg, WV 25405
www.ChristianPublish.com

Cover Design: Jay Cookingham

Printed in the United States of America and the United Kingdom

Table of Contents

6. Ways and Means of God's Action........................ 87

7. The Christian Family..................................... 121

1. Christianity

Ask any number of people, Christians and non-Christians alike, the question, "What is Christianity?" and you will get any number of answers. Christianity is not just one religion among many. Rather, true Christianity is not a religion at all. Therefore, a person who wishes to become a Christian does not go about it in the same manner as someone who wishes to become a member of a religion. One can access religion through the physical mind, whereas Christianity can only be accessed through the spirit, the human spirit. Human beings have a natural, physical nature and a spiritual nature. The natural nature has a physical mind and a physical body, and the spiritual nature has a spiritual mind and a spiritual body or form. The physical nature is only seen by the physical eyes, and the spiritual nature is only seen by the spiritual eyes. To access a religion or to become a member of any religion, only your physical nature has to be involved. But to become a Christian, your spiritual nature has to be involved.

"Jesus answered, 'I tell you the truth, no one can enter the kingdom of God unless he is born of water and the Spirit. Flesh gives birth to the flesh [physical nature] but the Spirit gives birth to spirit [spiritual nature]'" (John 3:5–6 NIV). To become a member of a religion you have to accept and live by its belief system, but to become a Christian, your total human nature; spirit, mind and body must be born from above, born again, born of God. Your spiritual nature is the key to that new creation.

Jesus Christ, the author of Christianity, commented on this.

> Just at that time, filled with joy by the Holy Spirit, he said, "I bless you Father, Lord of heaven and of earth, for hiding these things from the learned and the clever and revealing them to little children. Yes Father, for that is what it pleased you to do" (Luke 10:21 NJB).

Christianity derives its name from Jesus Christ, the Son of God. Its members are called Christians. They are followers and disciples of Christ. A disciple is a person who believes in and helps to spread the ideas and the teachings of Jesus Christ. A Christian is far more than a disciple in the ordinary sense. To be a Christian in reality and not just by name, the disciple must be in Christ (the disciple's responsibility and his doing), and Christ in him (Jesus Christ's responsibility and His doing). When one becomes a Christ-like person, Christ is formed in the believer. "My children, I am going through the pains of giving birth to you all over again, until Christ is formed in you" (Galatians 4:19 NJB).

"So for anyone who is in Christ there is a new creation: the old order is gone and a new being is there to see" (2 Corinthians 5:17 NJB).

To remain a Christian, one must abide in Jesus Christ. "Remain in me, as I in you. As a branch cannot bear fruit all by itself, unless it remains part of the vine, neither can you unless you remain in me" (John 15:4 NJB). A true Christian thinks like Jesus, acts like Jesus and has His character. He becomes His hands, His heart, His ears, His mouth, His eyes and His feet. The Christian is His representative here on the earth and is called to reflect His glory.

> "And all of us, with our unveiled faces like mirrors reflecting the glory of the Lord, are being transformed into the image that we reflect in brighter and brighter glory; this is the working of the Lord who is the Spirit" (2 Corinthians 3:18 NJB).

"I have given them the glory you gave to me, that they may be one as we are one" (John 17:22 NJB).

"In the same way your light must shine in people's sight, so that, seeing your good works, they may give praise to your Father in heaven" (Matthew 5:16 NJB). To give glory to God is to recognize His omnipotence, His omniscience, His omnipresence, His eternal love, and His divinity; to recognize who He is and to do His will, the will of God. The glory is the tangible manifested splendor and majesty of God in brightness and fire. To give glory to God is to recognize His omnipotence, His omniscience, His omnipresence, His eternal love, His divinity, to recognize who He is and by doing His will, the will of God, in your life.

Christianity is visible in the natural world even though God's kingdom is not of this world. "My kingdom is not of this world" (John 18:36 NIV). Christianity is lived in the supernatural realm, affecting spirit, mind and body. The mode of operation is the love-faith mode, God's mode of operation, in contrast to the hate-fear mode, which is Satan's mode of operation. True Christianity is a totally different reality; it is the true reality of humankind.

The Love-Faith Mode of Operation

Above all, God is love. He is the source of all love. His primary need is to love and to be loved in return. He longs for fellowship, for a constant loving relationship, for total communion. According to this principle, He created men and women. So men and women's purpose is to love God and their fellow men and women, and to be loved in return by God and their fellow men and women. God created humankind in such a way as to fulfill perfectly His purpose and intent. God is not insecure, but He made Himself vulnerable, because of the great love He has for His children. He can be grieved and suffer pain. "The Lord was grieved that he had made man on the earth, and his heart was filled with pain" (Genesis 6:6 NIV).

"And do not grieve the Holy Spirit of God, with whom you were sealed for the day of redemption" (Ephesians 4:30 NIV).

The word faith has many meanings in the English language. The context in which the word faith is used does not always tell us what the meaning of faith is. Therefore, it is very important to have a good understanding of the meanings of the word faith, especially when it concerns the Bible.

Here are the most commonly used faith expressions. To keep faith or to break faith means to keep a promise or to break a promise. Acting in good faith means being honest and sincere. Acting in bad faith means being dishonest and insincere. Faith can mean trust. One can trust a person, but not necessarily believe what that person says or does is true. Faith also can mean to believe. One can believe what a person says and does is true. Trusting and believing are two different things. Most confusion stems from three additional meanings of faith. They are faith (belief system), the measure of faith and true faith.

Faith as a Belief System

We say a certain person is a man or a woman of the faith—the Christian faith, the Moslem faith, the Hindu faith, etc. It means that person is a member of a particular religion or, for the Christian faith, that man or woman is a Christian. For Christians, Jesus Christ is the author and the perfecter of the Christian faith system. "Let us fix our eyes on Jesus, the author and perfecter of our faith" (Hebrews 12:2 NIV).

Faith as the Measure of Faith

Every human being has been given the measure of faith, not a measure of faith, but the measure of faith. A measure of faith would suggest any kind of a measure, but the measure of faith suggests the same for everybody.

"For by the grace given to me I say to every one of you: Do not think
of yourself more highly than you ought, but rather think of yourself
with sober judgment, in accordance with the measure of faith God
has given you" (Romans 12:3 NIV).

What is the measure of faith? The measure of faith is the faculty enabling a person to have faith. It is built into the human spirit. It is not a matter of size. Let's use a natural example to illustrate how the measure of faith functions.

A child is born with all the brain cells he or she will ever have. The child doesn't grow new brain cells. The vast majority of these brain cells are not functioning at birth, and that's why we are able to modulate, or you could say program, the brain and bring it to full maturity. Unless the brain of a child is specifically stimulated, his or her brain cells start dying off, and they never regrow. To build strong muscles, you need to train very hard. Olympic competitors can testify to that. Have you ever had a broken or injured leg or arm? If so, you are well aware of how quickly your muscles lose their shape and strength for that particular member. This brings us to the natural law that says that function determines structure. Brain growth and development are pure products of use. The more you use the brain, the better it becomes.

At birth, we have all the brain cells we will ever have, so there will be no additional brain cells ever, but there will be more neurological connections. That's brain growth, which will never cease until we die. That brain growth does not happen by itself, but is mostly dependant on each of us. It is called neurological organization. What is neurological organization? When we stimulate a brain cell, we stimulate the growth of the connection.

The more connections in that system, the more efficient that system is. The more efficient that system is, the more function we have. The brain cells start out non-operative, but with stimulation they develop and become operational. The growth of a child's physical brain is a growth of those connections. Only three percent of the brain comprises brain cells, while ninety-seven percent includes brain connections (hundred billions versus hundred trillions). Who is in control of those connections? You and I, of course, because we are in control of our children's environment and ourselves.

The measure of faith is comparable to the brain cells. The brain cells are useless unless programmed; so is the measure of faith useless unless programmed. Programming the measure of faith is to exercise and activate the measure of faith. Function determines the structure of the measure of faith. The measure of faith is a faculty of the human spirit and is able to function regardless of the state of the spirit—alive or dead, born-of-God or not born-of-God. "In the same way, faith [the measure of faith] by itself, if it is not accompanied by action, is dead" (James 2:17 NIV). Once the measure of faith is exercised and activated, that person becomes a man or a woman of faith, of true faith.

Faith as True Faith

What is true faith? I added the word true in front of the word faith to make a positive distinction from all other faith meanings. True faith is the product of the measure of faith being exercised and activated. It is or it should be the operating system of the human spirit. Fear, doubt and unbelief are part of Satan's mode of operation, which excludes true faith. A person who operates in fear operates in Satan's mode.

True faith always reaches its goal, pleasing God, but doesn't always attain its promises on earth. "And without [true] faith it is impossible to please God, because anyone who comes to him must believe that he exists and that he rewards those who earnestly seek him" (Hebrews 11:6 NIV).

"All these people were still living by [true] faith when they died. They did not receive the things promised; they only saw them and welcomed them from a distance. And they admitted that they were aliens and strangers on earth" (Hebrews 11:13 NIV).

> "True faith does not come from murdering common sense. It is not a peculiar psychology developed with great effort by saints in caves and living on bread and water. It is not peculiar at all. It is natural. Doubt is peculiar—irrational in fact. It is the only thing that ever surprised Jesus" (Bonnke, 2003).

"The disciples went and woke him, saying, 'Master, Master, we're going to drown!' He got up and rebuked the wind and the ragging waters; the storm subsided, and all was calm. 'Where is your faith?' he asked his disciples" (Luke 8:24–25 NIV). Faith cannot be applied to what one sees. Anything one can prove is factual and true. True faith is a decision and action based on belief. True faith comes by hearing the Word of God. You must dip yourself—spirit, mind and body—into the absolute truth known to God, the Word of God. True faith is intelligence of the spirit; it is ability of the spirit and part of the spiritual intrapersonal intelligence.

"Now [true] faith is being sure of what we hope for and certain of what we do not see" (Hebrews 11:1 NIV).

> The apostles said to the Lord, "Increase our faith!"
> He replied, "If you have faith as small as a mustard seed, you
> can say to this mulberry tree, 'Be uprooted and planted in the sea,'
> and it will obey you" (Luke 17:5—6 NIV).

Both faith references apply to true faith. God cannot increase your true faith. You have to exercise and activate the measure of faith. No faith, lack of faith, little faith, great faith, having faith, finding faith, growing faith, living by faith and faith made complete all refer to true faith. True faith can be lived; in fact, every born-of-God believer must live it. True faith can grow and mature and can be made complete. "The righteous will live by faith" (Romans 1:17 NIV). When living by faith, true faith is made complete and becomes as easy as breathing air.
Faith is the born-of-God spirit's mode of operation. It is bound by neither time nor space. It operates in an eternal mode, in a different realm of reality. Faith is now. The physical nature of human beings operates in the material world. For faith to be manifest in that time and space constrained realm, faith needs the cooperation of the physical mind and body. Sometimes, when your spirit believes and says one thing, your mind believes and says another thing. When your body does the opposite of what your spirit believes, thinks and says, then faith is rendered void. There must be unity among the three: spirit, mind and body. Once that unity is achieved, the manifestation of the promise will come to pass in the material world. This divine faith is at its best.

Suppose a person has cancer, well documented by scores of medical professionals. God says in his word, "By his wounds we are healed" (Isaiah 53:5 NIV). "We are healed" is present tense, now. The healing of that cancer is already accomplished in the spiritual realm, but for that healing to be manifest in the physical body, the mind and the body must cooperate with the spirit.

The person with the cancer must say the things that are not as though they are: "I am healed, I am cancer free." It is not denying the fact of the cancer, and it is not a lie, but it is simply putting a spiritual law to work. You come in agreement with your spirit, and you declare that you are healed.

God created the heavens and the earth, including humankind, by speaking them into existence. "He is our father in the sight of God, in whom he believed—the God who gives life to the dead and calls things that are not as though they were" (Romans 4:17 NIV).

Do not say, "I have faith for healing or I have faith for money to pay the bills," but say, "I have faith in the healer, I have faith in the provider." To operate in the love-faith mode is a prerogative of a true Christian.

Christianity is life, eternal life, sonship and power, lived through its main principle, the love principle: Love for God, Love for people and love for enemies. That life in Jesus Christ has to be nourished daily, and the sonship with the heavenly Father has to translate into a daily, loving relationship with God the Father, God the Son and God the Holy Spirit. The end result will be power to destroy the works of the adversary and to implement God's kingdom here on the earth.

The Hate-Fear Mode of Operation

"Then Peter got down out of the boat, walked on the water and came towards Jesus. But when he saw the wind, he was afraid and, beginning to sink, cried out, 'Lord, save me!'" (Matthew 14:29–30 NIV). The moment Peter took his eyes off Jesus and focused on the circumstance, fear entered his spirit. Faith left and he sank. Fear and faith do not mix. Either you have faith or you have fear, but you cannot have both present at the same time.

Fear is everybody's enemy. Fear is an emotion, a powerful force. Fear is also a negative spiritual force. Fear is caused by expected evil or impending danger. The first reaction to a frightening stimulus is a violent contraction of all flexor muscles, especially in the abdominal region. A halt in breathing is soon followed by a whole series of vasomotor disturbances such as an accelerated pulse, sweating, even urination and defecation. The contraction of the flexors inhibits their antagonistic extensors or antigravity muscles. Thus no displacement occurs before the initial reaction is over. The frightened person freezes and is nailed to his place for a short time, giving the attacker a better chance by enabling him or her to pounce on a fixed target instead of a fleeting one. In the spirit, a similar reaction occurs leaving that person at the mercy of the devil. That's the reason why the devil, your enemy, "prowls around like a roaring lion looking for someone to devour" (1 Peter 5:8 NIV).

Fear does even greater damage, because no true faith is produced, and therefore nothing lasting is accomplished or attained, including the born-of-God experience. Evil spirits will do anything and everything to make you afraid. Once you operate in fear and not in faith, they will have power over you and God cannot help you. Monster movies, demonic dreams, psychics, witchcraft, Satan worship and the like have one thing in common. They all engender fear in you. That's the devil's first line of attack. Once fear takes hold, deception sets in, followed by death and total destruction. That's the way the devil always operates.

During the Second World War, the German dive-bombers, the Stukas, were equipped with horrifying sound-producing devices. When they attacked, they struck the enemy with terror and fear. The Belgians had a bastion, which was well fortified, that served as a strategic key to ward off the enemy with only one weak point—the sky. The Germans realized that and came up with an ingenious plan. They dropped parachute troops from the sky, but with a difference. Most of the troops were dummies and the sheer number of them created fear and havoc among the Belgians. The battle lasted only a few hours. Not too long after that lost battle, the king surrendered to Hitler. These are good examples of what fear can do in the natural realm, and the destruction in the spiritual realm is even greater. There are three hundred and sixty-five "fear nots" in the Bible, one for each day of the year.

Have we Christians deviated from the ideal? Have we failed in our Christian calling? Some of us are mired in controversy over doctrine, and still others have totally lost sight of their heavenly calling.

2. The Start of Christianity

The roots of Christianity go far back into Jewish history, long before Jesus Christ. In fact, Christian beliefs go as far back as the creation of Adam and Eve. The Old Testament era is a giant preparation, culminating in the coming of Jesus Christ, the Son of the living God. Through Him, what God has to say is revealed to humanity. He discipled a mere handful to propagate the Good News for the ages to come. Once taken up into heaven, He had to leave behind a structure that would guarantee that His mission would not be lost, but would extend to the ends of the world in the ages to come. That structure is the visible church, composed of members forming His mystical body, the body of Christ, of which He is the head. "...so in Christ we who are many form one body" (Romans 12:5 NIV).

"Now you are the body of Christ, and each one of you is a part of it" (1 Corinthians 12:27 NIV).

"And God placed all things under his feet and appointed him to be head over everything for the church, which is his body, the fullness of him who fills everything in every way" (Ephesians 1:22 NIV).

"And he is the head of the body, the church; he is the beginning and the firstborn from among the dead, so that in everything he might have supremacy" (Colossians 1:18 NIV).

Jesus chose a leader to head His church and the disciples. It was Peter, the Apostle. Every list of the disciples names him first. He had a big heart, a heart after God's own heart, and unlimited enthusiasm with many rough edges.

> "But what about you?" he asked, " Who do you say I am?"
>
> Simon Peter answered, "You are the Christ, the Son of the living God."
>
> Jesus replied, "Blessed are you, Simon son of Jonah, for this was not revealed to you by man, but by my Father in heaven. And I tell you that you are Peter, and on this rock I will build my church, and the gates of Hades will not overcome it. I will give you the keys of the kingdom of heaven; whatever you bind on earth will be bound in heaven, and whatever you loose on earth will be loosed in heaven" (Matthew 16:15–19 NIV).

Not too long afterwards, Peter disowned Jesus, his master, who previously had him appointed to the highest office any human being could reach.

Now Peter was sitting out in the courtyard, and a servant girl came to him. "You also were with Jesus of Galilee," she said.

But he denied it before them all. "I don't know what you're talking about," he said.

Then he went out to the gateway, where another girl saw him and said to the people there, "This fellow was with Jesus of Nazareth."

He denied it again, with an oath: "I don't know the man!"

After a little while, those standing around there went up to Peter and said, "Surely you are one of them, for your accent gives you away."

Then he began to call curses on himself and he swore to them, "I don't know the man!"

Immediately a rooster crowed. Then Peter remembered the word Jesus had spoken: "Before the rooster crows, you will disown me three times." And he went outside and wept bitterly (Matthew 26:69–75 NIV).

After His resurrection, Jesus appeared to His disciples and, on one occasion, He reinstated Peter.

When they had finished eating, Jesus said to Simon Peter, "Simon son of John, do you truly love me more than these?"

"Yes, Lord," he said, "you know that I love you."

Jesus said, "Feed my lambs."

Again Jesus said, "Simon son of John, do you truly love me?"

He answered, "Yes, Lord, you know that I love you." Jesus said, "Take care of my sheep."

The third time he said to him, "Simon son of John, do you love me?' Peter was hurt because Jesus asked him the third time, "Do you love me?"

He said, "Lord, you know all things: you know that I love you."

Jesus said, "Feed my sheep" (John 21:15–17 NIV).

Peter is given the task to feed the young Christians, to take care of the adult Christians, to nourish them and to bring them to maturity.

"And I tell you that you are Peter, and on this rock I will build my church, and the gates of Hades will not overcome it" (Matthew 16:18 NIV). This verse is causing a much-debated uproar among Protestants. They proclaim Jesus is the rock, not Peter.

And others say, Peter in Greek, *Petros,* is a mere pebble, and the church is built upon Peter's pebble revelation, "You are the Christ the Son of the living God" (Matthew 16:15 NIV). Jesus cannot be the rock. He did not say, "I am the rock and upon this rock I will build my church." It really does not make sense. No, He is talking about Peter, the rock upon which He will build his church.

The Bible tells us that Jesus is the bridegroom and the church is the bride—two different entities. If Jesus were the rock, then there would be only one entity. The bridegroom and the bride cannot be the same person.

God delights in using the foolish things of this world to confound the wise, and the fragile things to manifest His power. The Bible says, "For my power is made perfect in weakness" (2 Corinthians 12:9 NIV).

"...and the gates of Hades will not overcome it" (Matthew 16:18 NIV). If Jesus were the rock, this statement would be superfluous. Satan is no match for God Almighty. Do not insult Him by saying He is the rock.

There are Bible verses where Jesus and the Father are depicted as a rock. Those verses have no connection with Matthew 16:18. The word rock is often used to convey the meaning of something solid and stable that cannot be moved, something you can rely upon. Psalm 89:26 (NJB) says, "He will cry to me. You are my Father, my God, the rock of my salvation!"

1 Corinthians 10:3–4 (NJB) states, "They all ate the same spiritual food and drank the same spiritual drink; for they drank from the spiritual rock that followed them, and that rock was Christ."

Jesus changed Simon's name to Peter. Peter is the English name for rock, a massive stone. The New Testament was written in Koine Greek, in which both *Petros* (masculine) and *Petra* (feminine) mean rock, not pebble. The Greek word for pebble is *lithos*. In Attic Greek, centuries before Jesus Christ, Greek poets used *Petros* and *Petra* interchangeably as synonyms for either pebble or rock.

Jesus spoke Aramaic. Some of those words are preserved for us in the Gospels. *"Eloi,Eloi lama sabachthani?"* (Matthew 27:46 NIV). This is not Greek, but Aramaic, and it means, "My God, my God, why have you forsaken me?"

Most people, when in a dramatic life-threatening situation, almost always use their native language. In Galatians and in 1 Corinthians we find the Aramaic form of Simon's new name *Kepha* eight times preserved for us. English translations show the word as Cephas. *Kepha* means large, massive rock, not a pebble, which would be *evna*. The French word for Peter is *Pierre* and for pebble is *cailloux*. Peter is the rock no matter how one looks at it, and it will not change a two thousand year old reality.

There is a city called Petra, the capitol of Edom and later of Nabatea, situated about eighty kilometers south of the Dead Sea. What is amazing about that city is that most of its buildings and tombs are cut out into the rose-red rock cliffs of the area, a massive rocky city indeed.

One very significant aspect of Jesus' instructions to His apostles and disciples was His command to wait for the Holy Spirit before they would do anything; before they would launch the new church. Jesus appeared to the disciples over a period of forty days. On one occasion, while He was eating with them, He gave them this command: "Do not leave Jerusalem, but wait for the gift my Father promised, which you have heard me speak about. For John baptized with water, but in a few days you will be baptized with the Holy Spirit" (Acts 1:4–5 NIV).

"But you will receive power when the Holy Spirit comes on you; and you will be my witnesses in Jerusalem, and in all Judea and Samaria, and to the ends of the earth" (Acts 1:8 NIV).

The key to success for any Christian, the church and even for Jesus Himself while here on the earth was and is the Holy Spirit.

The Holy Spirit in the Life of Jesus

Jesus the Son of God, while walking here on earth, was perfect man, stripped of all godly attributes.

> Who, being in very nature God, did not consider equality with God
> something to be grasped, but made himself nothing, taking the very
> nature of a servant, being made in human likeness. And being found

in appearance as a man, he humbled himself and became obedient to death—even death on a cross! (Philippians 2:6–8 NIV). He could not perform any miracles except through the power of the Holy Spirit, and He was completely and totally dependent on the Holy Spirit for His mission here on earth. Pause for a moment and think about it; how Jesus Himself had to rely constantly on the Holy Spirit. How much more must we –imperfect as we are, yet replacing Jesus here on earth—rely on the Holy Spirit.

Begotten of the Holy Spirit

"The Holy Spirit will come upon you, and the power of the Most High will overshadow you. So the holy one to be born will be called the Son of God" (Luke 1:35 NIV). Jesus was conceived by the Holy Spirit in the womb of Mary. He is the one who will form Jesus in you, if you let Him. You take on the character of Jesus and become His representative here on the earth.

Paul is telling us that he no longer lives, but Christ lives in him. "I have been crucified with Christ and I no longer live, but Christ lives in me" (Galatians 2:20 NIV). Once Jesus is formed in you, you will not resist the Holy Spirit any longer but live in total surrender and complete obedience to your heavenly Father.

Baptized

> I saw the Spirit come down from heaven as a dove and remain on him. I would not have known him, except that the one who sent me to baptize with water told me, "The man on whom you see the Spirit come down and remain is he who will baptize with the Holy Spirit" (John 1:32–33 NIV).

It is worth noticing that the Holy Spirit remained upon Jesus all His earthly life. " and the Holy Spirit descended on him in bodily form like a dove. And a voice came from heaven: 'You are my Son, whom I love; with you I am well pleased'" (Luke 3:22 NIV).

The Spirit is given to Jesus without limit

For the one whom God has sent speaks the words of God, for God gives the Spirit without limit" (John 3:34 NIV).

Jesus was taught by the Holy Spirit
> A shoot will come up from the stump of Jesse; from his roots a Branch will bear fruit. The Spirit of the Lord will rest on him—the Spirit of wisdom and of understanding, the Spirit of counsel and of power, the Spirit of knowledge and of the fear of the Lord (Isaiah 11:1–2 NIV).

Through the Holy Spirit, Jesus brought justice to the nations
"Here is my servant, whom I uphold, my chosen one in whom I delight; I will put my Spirit on him and he will bring justice to the nations" (Isaiah 42:1 NIV).

Anointed to preach
> The Spirit of the Lord is on me, because he has anointed me to preach good news to the poor. He has sent me to proclaim freedom for the prisoners and recovery of sight for the blind, to release the oppressed... (Luke 4:18 NIV).

The anointing qualified Jesus for the service to which God had called him.

Casting out demons
"But if I drive out demons by the Spirit of God, then the kingdom of God has come upon you" (Matthew 12:28 NIV).

Servant
"Here is my servant whom I have chosen, the one I love, in whom I delight; I will put my Spirit on him, and he will proclaim justice to the nations" (Matthew 12:18 NIV).

Led by the Holy Spirit
"Jesus, full of the Holy Spirit, returned from the Jordan and was led by the Spirit in the desert" (Luke 4:1 NIV).

To declare the transgression and sin of Israel
"But as for me, I am filled with power, with the Spirit of the Lord, and with justice and might, to declare to Jacob his transgression, to Israel his sin" (Micah 3:8 NIV).

Joy through the Holy Spirit
"At that time Jesus, full of joy through the Holy Spirit, said, 'I praise you, Father...'" (Luke 10:21 NIV).

Gives instructions

"...until the day he was taken up to heaven, after giving instructions through the Holy
Spirit to the apostles he had chosen" (Acts 1:2 NIV).

Offered himself

"How much more, then, will the blood of Christ, who through the eternal Spirit offered himself unblemished to God, cleanse our consciences from acts that lead to death, so that we may serve the living God!" (Hebrews 9:14 NIV).

Raised from the dead

"And if the Spirit of him who raised Jesus from the dead is living in you, he who raised Christ from the dead will also give life to your mortal bodies through his Spirit, who lives in you" (Romans 8:11 NIV)

Vindicated

"He appeared in a body, was vindicated by the Spirit, was seen by angels, was preached among the nations, was believed on in the world, was taken up in glory" (1 Timothy 3:16 NIV). Jesus, the Son of Man, triumphed and fulfilled his mission perfectly. The previous Bible verses leave no doubt whatsoever that one cannot separate the Holy Spirit from the life of Jesus here on earth.

The same work that the Holy Spirit did in the life of Jesus, He, the Holy Spirit can do in our lives. That's the reason Jesus said, "The same work I did you will do and even greater works you will do, because I am going to the Father" (John 14:12 paraphrased). The determining factors for doing greater works are the Holy Spirit and the fact that we live in the end times, when greater works are on God's agenda.

Day one of the Church of Jesus Christ was the day of Pentecost.

> Then they returned to Jerusalem from the hill called the Mount of Olives, a Sabbath day's walk from the city. When they arrived, they went upstairs to the room where they were staying. Those present were Peter, John, James, and Andrew; Philip and Thomas, Bartholomew and Matthew; James son of Alphaeus and Simon the Zealot, and Judas son of James. They all joined together constantly in prayer, along with the women and Mary the mother of Jesus, and with his brothers.

In those days Peter stood up among the believers (a group numbering about a hundred and twenty)" (Acts 1:12–15 NIV).

When the day of Pentecost came, they were all together in one place. Suddenly a sound like the blowing of a violent wind came from heaven and filled the whole house where they were sitting. They saw what seemed to be tongues of fire that separated and came to rest on each of them. All of them were filled with the Holy Spirit and began to speak in other tongues as the Spirit enabled them (Acts 2:1–4 NIV).

The church of Jesus Christ was birthed with about one hundred and twenty apostles and disciples, men, women and children. One thing to remember was they were all together in one accord, in perfect unity. That gives us a second key for a successful church. "Those who accepted his message were baptized, and about three thousand were added to their number that day" (Acts 2:41 NIV).

Characteristics of the New Church

The church Jesus Christ founded has four major characteristics. The church is apostolic, catholic, one and holy.

Apostolic

Jesus not only appointed Peter, the rock, as leader of the apostles, but also head of the church and gave him special powers as well. "I will give you the keys of the kingdom of heaven; whatever you bind on earth will be bound in heaven, and whatever you loose on earth will be loosed in heaven" (Matthew 16:19 NIV).

The church is apostolic because Jesus set the apostles to be its first leaders, and their successors were to be its future leaders. The apostles were the first bishops, and since the first century, there has been an unbroken line of bishops faithfully handing down what the apostles taught the first Christians in Scripture and oral tradition. Early Christians' writings prove the first Christians were thoroughly catholic in belief and practice and looked to the successors of the apostles as their leaders. What these first Christians believed is still believed by the apostolic church today.

Catholic

The church Jesus established was known by its most common title, the Catholic Church at least as early as the year 107, when Ignatius of Antioch used that title to describe the one church Jesus founded. Apparently, the title was old in Ignatius' time, which means it probably went all the way back to the time of the apostles. Catholic originally meant according to true church, as distinct from all others religious groups. Secondly, it also means universal. The word catholic is so strong that if a Christian denies being catholic he denies believing the doctrine of Jesus Christ handed down by the apostles. "Therefore go and make disciples of all nations, baptizing them in the name of the Father, and of the Son and of the Holy Spirit, and teaching them to obey everything I have commanded you" (Matthew 28:19–20 NIV).

For two thousand years the Catholic Church has carried out this mission, preaching the good news that Christ died for all men and that He wants all of us to be members of His universal family. The Catholic Church extends to every nation and race, is neither national nor ethnic, but truly universal. "There is neither Jew nor Greek, slave nor free, male nor female, for you are all one in Christ Jesus" (Galatians 3:28 NIV).

Holy

The church is made holy by Jesus Christ.

> Husbands, love your wives, just as Christ loved the church and gave himself up for her to make her holy, cleansing her by the washing with water through the word, and to present her to himself as a radiant church, without stain or wrinkle or any other blemish, but holy and blameless" (Ephesians 5:25–27 NIV).

Not all the members are always holy, there are good and bad members in the church and not all the members will be saved eternally. "Not everyone who says to me, 'Lord, Lord,' will enter the kingdom of heaven, but only he who does the will of my Father who is in heaven" (Matthew 7:21 NIV).

The church itself is holy because it is a source of holiness for its members. The six-fold ministry in the church, mentioned in Ephesians, is the means by which its members attain to the whole measure of the fullness of Christ.

> "It was he who gave some to be apostles, some to be prophets, some to be evangelists, and some to be pastors and teachers, to prepare

God's people for works of service, [the ministry of helps] so that the body of Christ may be built up until we all reach unity in the faith and in the knowledge of the Son of God and become mature, attaining to the whole measure of the fullness of Christ" (Ephesians 4:11–13 NIV).

One

Jesus Christ established only one church, and that is the Catholic Church. It is a visible organization existing almost two thousand years. The church faced tremendous opposition over the years but is still in existence and more vibrant than ever, a testimony to its divine origin.

According to the Bible the church is the bride of Christ. Jesus can have but one spouse, and that spouse is the Catholic Church.

Any other Christian churches like the Baptist, the Anglican, the Pentecostal, etc. are actually offshoots of the original Catholic Church. Some are offshoots of an offshoot. They are still part of the one church Jesus founded, even though they are not of the same fold. But one thing they must have in common is but one set of doctrines taught by Jesus and handed down by the apostles. The church's official teachers—the pope and the bishops united with him—have never changed any doctrine. Over the centuries, as doctrines are examined more fully, the church comes to clarify, to express and to understand them more deeply, but it never understands them to mean the opposite of what they once meant. "I have other sheep that are not of this sheep pen. I must bring them also. They too listen to my voice, and there shall be one flock and one shepherd" (John 10:16 NIV).

3. Peter and His Successors as the Spiritual Fathers of the Church

Peter and his successors are the spiritual fathers of all Christians, both Catholics and Protestants including their legitimate offshoots. As the head of the church they hold the most powerful office any man can hold. The successor to Peter as bishop of Rome is affectionately called papa or pope. The world's other bishops are successors to the apostles in general. The pope, as vicar of Christ, is the head of His church under the guidance of the Holy Spirit. A vicar is a representative. Actually, every believer is a representative of Jesus Christ here on earth. Among the many titles a pope holds, I like servant of the servants of God the best. Years ago, I was a catholic monk with a serious complaint. Getting nowhere, I wrote to the pope (Pope Paul VI). He wrote me back promising to pray for me. He also sent me a gold medal of his and fifty dollars. I was impressed. Very few people can claim that the pope prayed for them personally. Not only did the pope pray for me, but in every Catholic Church all over the world all believers pray for the intentions of the pope, and that included me at that time. Just imagine, over one billion people praying for you—just mind-boggling. My wife thinks I needed those prayers badly.

"Instead, the greatest among you should be like the youngest, and the one who rules like the one who serves" (Luke 22:26 NIV). The pope who rules is the one who serves.

He is also the one to strengthen the other bishops in their faith (belief system) ensuring that they proclaim the Word of God and make decisions based on the Truth. "Simon, Simon, Satan has asked to sift you as wheat. But I have prayed for you, Simon, that your faith may not fail. And when you have turned back, strengthen your brothers" (Luke 22: 31–32 NIV). He is also the chief shepherd of the church of Jesus Christ.

Jesus chose Peter and his successors to teach and govern, not as dictators, but as loving pastors and fathers. Paul wrote in 1 Corinthians 4:15, "Even though you have ten thousand guardians in Christ, you do not have many fathers, for in Christ Jesus I became your father through the gospel" (NIV).

Many non-Catholic believers do not hold a kind image of the pope and the papacy. It is true some popes of the past were not worthy to hold the office of the pope.

Judas, the apostle shared in Jesus' ministry. He was called and appointed by Jesus Christ Himself, yet he betrayed Him. Every man and every woman make their own decisions in life. Our focus should not be on the unworthy ones, but on the worthy ones. The unworthy ones give us a good example how not to do it. A great deal of the problem of unworthy popes had to do with the way they were elected, who appointed them and the historical circumstances of the world they lived in. The interference of the state in church affairs and vice versa is probably the most serious one.

> So they proposed two men: Joseph called Barsabbas (also known as Justus) and Matthias. Then they prayed, "Lord you know everyone's heart. Show us which one of these two you have chosen to take over this apostolic ministry, which Judas left to go where he belongs." Then they cast lots, and the lot fell to Matthias; so he was added to the eleven apostles (Acts 1:23–26 NIV).

These verses of the Bible show us how for the first few centuries the successors of Peter and the other apostles were selected and appointed. They relied heavily on the Holy Spirit and on their knowledge of the characters of the prospective candidates. The Holy Spirit must be in charge in the selection of a pope, a bishop, a priest or a minister. In time, the worldly system infiltrated church politics. The Early Church became rich, everything was put in common and there was no need among them. "All the believers were together and had everything in common. Selling their possessions and goods, they gave to anyone as he had need" (Acts 2:44–45 NIV).

Severe persecutions arose and all the property of the Christians was seized. Emperor Gallienus (260) who succeeded Decius and Valerian entertained a much more friendly relationship with the Christians. He issued an edict that not only brought peace to the church for forty years, but restored to it all the property that had been seized in early persecutions. Unfortunately, more persecutions followed under Diocletian and Constantine. Constantine contracted leprosy. Later he embraced Christianity and was healed. Out of gratitude he heaped honors and gifts upon the pope. The Lateran palace, hitherto an imperial residence, was given over to the church to provide Rome's bishop with his first permanent home. He also built the basilica now known as Saint John Lateran Church. It quickly became clear that good relations between church and state, between pope and emperor, were vital for both. From that time on, church and state became strange bedfellows. Constant interference between the two became the way of life for centuries to come. A good example of that is the Council of Nicaea, which was convened by Emperor

Constantine the Great in 325, and not by the pope. But the close relationship between emperor and pope meant a lot more than restoration of property to Christians and the construction of churches. Great privileges granted to them distinguished them from all other belief systems.

Almost sixty years later, Emperor Theodosius called a general council at Constantinople in May 381. Theodosius made a personal appearance at the opening. He invited only bishops from the eastern part of the empire. The Italians were absent, notably Pope Damasus, who did not even send a representative. The long and painful road of the church in the shadow of worldly powers began. With the acquisition of lands and cities in and outside Italy, the need for defense of such states became a necessity. Those states are known as the Papal States. They were the central Italian temporal realm of the popes from 754 to 1870. They generally included the modern Italian regions of Lazio, Umbria, Marche and Romagna, part of Emilia. In 756, Pepin the Short, a Frankish ruler, granted the exarch state of Ravenna to Pope Stephen II, establishing the pope's temporal power. The country surrounding Avignon was part of the Papal States, and in the middle of the fourteenth century the pope purchased the town from Naples.

Some popes became warriors with armies of fifty thousand and more. Pope John VIII built up his own navy. In 876, under his personal command, they captured almost twenty Saracen ships and freed some six hundred captives. He also bred horses for his cavalry. One nobleman, Gandulf, lost his fortress to Pope Alexandre III (1154–1159). Later the villa of Castel Gandolfo, which now serves as the summer residence of the popes, was built by Carlo Moderna (1556–1629) on the instruction of Pope Urban VIII. Pope Urban VI (1378–1389) occasionally led his armies into battle himself. As if the administration and the defense of the Papal States were not enough worry for the popes, this area was plagued with a famine in 1648. The Papal States were largely annexed by France between 1797 and 1809. They were restored in 1814, only to be annexed to Italy in 1860 and 1870.

The Kingdom of Piedmont, in the north of Italy, had the aspiration of a united Italy. The only obstacle to Piedmont's realization was the presence in Rome of a French garrison. In 1870, after the defeat of France in the Franco-Prussian War, Napoleon III fell from power, and the garrison in Rome was withdrawn. Pope Pius IX ordered his tiny army to surrender, and on September 20, 1870, the Papal States fell forever. But it was not until 1929 that the long-standing problems between the kingdom of Italy and the Holy See were resolved through the Lateran Treaty. The pope was left as sovereign of the Vatican City State, with extra territorial rights over some buildings in Rome and Castel Gandolfo, and to top it off, with a huge financial settlement.

Finally, the pope could dedicate his entire energy for the spiritual good of the church and not be tangled down by worldly aspirations. The Vatican City State, with an area of 0.4 square kilometers, is home to about one thousand residents. There is no freedom of religion there; therefore, it cannot sign the UN Declaration of Human Rights. In theory at least, it is the most absolute dictatorship in the world. Once asked, "How many are working in the Vatican?" Pope John XXIII replied, "About half." There are about 2250 workers.

One of the reasons for a constant entanglement of emperors and popes was the bestowing on worldly monarchs the title of Holy Roman Emperor by the popes. The first such coronation was of Charlemagne by Pope Leo III (795–816). It took place on Christmas Day (800). The last emperor to be crowned as such was Charles V (1500–1558), but the title stayed in use until 1806, when the Hapsburg family, which had appropriated it, finally abandoned it.

Pope John XII needed help to repel King Berengar of Italy, who was destined to take over Rome. So he turned to Otto I, King of Saxony. He came to Rome on John's call and was crowned Holy Roman Emperor on February 2, 962. Otto liberated the states of the church seized by the King of Italy, but he did so by re-conquering them for himself and making their inhabitants his own subjects. The Holy Emperors did not just meddle in the territorial affairs of the church, but most of all in the elections of the popes, for their own interests or the interests of their families and offspring. So did some of the popes themselves. The interference of outsiders in the elections of church officials is called investiture. It was in effect in early Middle Ages (476–1450). Investiture was an important feature of the feudal system. It was the lord's or sovereign's right to make appointments to church offices, thus subjecting churchmen, such as bishops, abbots and priests, to the control of a lay person. Often no concern was paid to the qualifications necessary for assuming these responsible positions. Holy orders were conferred on ignorant, unworthy people. Ambitious men chose the clerical state to obtain preferential treatment and advancement. These church opportunists sometimes claimed the right to marry. A change in attitude came in 769 in the form of an election decree that no layman was to intervene in the choosing of a new pope and that only cardinal priests of the Roman Church could become Bishop of Rome. Cardinal, at first, was not a title of honor, but indicated a role in the church. Bishops and priests normally served the church in which they were ordained, but in Rome the parish churches had to supply priests for the Lateran Basilica, Saint Peter's, Saint Paul's, Outside the Walls, and Sancta Maria Maggiore. The bishops and priests who performed their duties outside the church of their ordination were called cardinals.

Another major step for a proper pope election came with the synod of 1059. It laid down that in the future, cardinal bishops were to nominate a candidate for the papacy, lesser cardinals were to approve him and the clergy and the people of Rome were to accept him. The choice had to come from among the clergy of the Roman Church and the emperor was to have no more than a formal right of approval. It was an attempt to free the papacy from political interference. The gathering of the cardinals was called consistory, taken from Byzantine practice, not from Roman.

The synod decree was not practiced in 1073. Hildebrand, who took the name Gregory VII, was acclaimed as pope by the people of Rome. He was notably convinced that only through a complete separation of church and state could the church rid itself of the ills that afflicted it. The most blatant sign of state interference in the church affairs, he believed, was the problem of investiture. So, in February 1075, Pope Gregory VII issued a decree forbidding the lay investiture of clerics. Thomas Becket, Archbishop of Canterbury, was murdered by Henry II, because of Becket's opposition to interference in elections to bishoprics.

In 1179, bishops, abbots and heads of religious orders met in council in the Lateran basilica. They determined that the pope was to be elected by a two-thirds majority of the cardinals, without reference to the clergy or the people of Rome and without consultation with the emperor.

Before he passed away in August 1241, Pope Gregory IX made arrangements with the senator of Rome, Matteo Rossi Orsini, to prevent Emperor Frederic II from getting any ideas to appoint a pope himself. After Gregory had died, Orsini arrested all the cardinals he could find and imprisoned them in the Septizonian palace with the coffin of the pope. Furthermore, the cardinals were subjected to all kinds of discomfort, not the least of which was a spear struck up the mattress as soon as a cardinal would lay down to sleep. No wonder one cardinal died and the remaining cardinals had to live with two corpses. A new pope was speedily chosen: Celestine IV. Even today the cardinals are still confined during the conclave.

Pope Martin V (1417–1431), through the recommendations of a reforming council he had implemented, made the College of Cardinals into an internationally representative body. He introduced new rules to guarantee his control over its members and their way of life.

In time, monarchs and lay people lost their grip on the election of popes and clerics, but they found another way of influencing a pope's election. They interfered in the process of getting a person made a cardinal.

Giovanni de Medici, at the age of thirteen, became the youngest cardinal ever, at the instigation of his father. Even the pope was embarrassed and insisted on keeping the elevation secret for three years. Cardinal Giovanni, commander of the papal troupes at the battle of Ravenna, was elected pope and took the name of Leo X (1513–1521). Pope Paul III (1534–1549) made three of his grandsons cardinals, at the ages of fourteen, fifteen and sixteen, and Pope Sixtus V (1585–1590) elevated his fifteen year old to the cardinal office.

Benedict XIV was elected pope, after 255 ballots, in August 1740. The conclave lasted six months and two cardinals died during its course in the hot summer heat. But it was not until Pope Pius X was elected pope on August 4, 1903 that the last vestige of lay investiture in the election of a pope was definitely abolished. Austria, a Catholic power, had exercised its traditional right of veto against one of the foremost candidates during the conclave that followed Leo XIII's death. It was the last time such a thing was to happen. In 1952 Angelo Giuseppe Roncalli was made a cardinal by Pope Pius XII. At the time, Roncalli was the nuncio of France. Later Cardinal Roncalli became Pope John Paul the XXIII. His love, his humility and his humor made him greatly loved and respected by all. The President of the French Republic, who was an atheist, insisted on exercising the ancient privilege of the French kings, by bestowing on the nuncio his red biretta, the sign of his rank in the church. It was in no way a sign of state interference in church affairs, but a remarkable respectful gesture showing how church and state can cooperate in a positive way.

Looking back, one realizes that it is a real miracle the church did not go astray, nor did it falter in any way, even though some of its popes were not the Holy Spirit's choice. Today, we see the Catholic Church, the Church of Jesus Christ, flourishing like never before, thanks to God's grace and His promise made to Peter that the gates of hell would not prevail.

The negative and the worldly easily captivate our attention, whereas the positive and the spiritual are less visible but even more important. The popes influenced the church and the world for two thousand years, mostly in a positive way, and still do so to this very day. The inhabitants of the earth benefit greatly from that influence. Sometimes a simple decision of a pope results in a great lasting impact. In the fifteenth and sixteenth centuries Portugal and Spain were great naval powers. They sailed to the New World, not just to conquer, but also to evangelize. To avoid rivalry between the two, the pope drew a line on the world map from the North Pole to the South Pole, just west of the Azores. All to the west of the line, he said, belongs to Spain; all to the east belongs to Portugal. This explains why Brazil is a Portuguese-speaking country today and the rest of Latin America is Spanish. By papal commission, the kings of Spain and Portugal were responsible to evangelize the conquered lands. The church expected the kings to send out missionaries and appoint bishops to the newly acquired lands.

Christianity is responsible for the creation of universities (approximately 1140), and many popes either created universities, or at least promoted this new kind of higher educational institutions. Boniface VIII (1294–1303) founded the University of Rome, and Clement V (1305–1314) established the universities at Orleans and Perugia. He established chairs of Hebrew, Arabic and Syriac at Paris, Bologna, Oxford and Salamanca. Innocent XI (1676–1689), who tried to abolish slavery in Africa with little success, established universities in Latin America and the Philippines.

The popes have spiritual weapons at their disposal to defend the integrity of the Christian belief system, to protect church property, clergy and the faithful from harm. The three major weapons are the interdict, excommunication and infallibility.

The Interdict

The interdict falls upon a whole nation, while excommunication is aimed at individuals. The interdict suspends public worship, withdraws the sacraments, with the exception of baptism and extreme unction, from the lands of disobedient rulers.

Excommunication

Excommunication is the most serious censure of the Catholic Church. The excommunicated person is excluded from church offices (priests, bishops and lay persons), from the communion of the faithful and from divine service except preaching and is provided no Christian burial. There are different degrees of excommunication: *vivandi,* when the faithful are forbidden to associate with them and *tolerati* when the faithful may still associate with them.

Excommunication is imposed to heretics, apostates, schismatics and those who are reading or retaining books of formal heretics, apostates and schismatics wherein these sins are defended, or other books condemned in apostolic letters.

To all who procure an abortion, including the mother and all cooperators, excommunication is also imposed. Abortion is murder pure and simple—no ifs and no buts. Psalm 51:5 declares, "Surely I was sinful at birth, sinful from the time my mother conceived me" (NIV). Sinfulness is a spiritual rather than a physical condition. God gives a spirit to every human being at conception.

The spirit is the life-principle of the human body. "The body without the spirit is dead" (James 2:26 NIV). At conception a child's body is alive and growing.

In 1995, Pope John Paul II made a declaration regarding the church's teaching on abortion.

> [It] is unchanged and unchangeable. Therefore, by the authority which Christ conferred upon Peter and his successors … I declare that direct abortion, that is, abortion willed as an end or as a means, always constitutes a grave moral disorder, since it is the deliberate killing of an innocent human being. This doctrine is based upon the natural law and upon the written word of God, transmitted by the Church's tradition and taught by the ordinary and universal magisterium. No circumstance, no purpose, no law whatsoever can ever make licit an act which is intrinsically illicit, since it is contrary to the law of God, which is written in every human heart, knowable by reason itself and proclaimed by the Church" (Evangelium Vitae, 1995).

Other noteworthy causes for excommunication include marrying before a heretical minister, agreeing to bring up children outside the church ["And if anyone causes one of these little ones who believe in me to sin, it would be better for him to be thrown into the sea with a large millstone tied around his neck" (Mark 9:42 NIV)], striking clerics or nuns, ["Do not touch my anointed ones; do my prophets no harm"

(Psalm 105:15 NIV)], and publishing books of Scripture or commentaries on it without due permission.

Excommunication seems harsh, but the teaching of the Bible is harsher still.
> When you are assembled in the name of our Lord Jesus and I am with you in spirit, and the power of our Lord Jesus is present, hand this man over to Satan, so that the sinful nature may be destroyed and his spirit saved on the day of the Lord. Expel the wicked man from among you" (1 Corinthians 5:4, 5 and 13 NIV).

The censure can be lifted at any time, if the excommunicated person repents, changes his ways and recants.

In 1981 a Moslem extremist Mohamad Ali Agca shot Pope John Paul II twice, from nine feet away. A nun tugged the aggressor's jacket, which spoiled a perfect aim. Thereby she saved the pope from being killed. One bullet hit his stomach, the other his right hand. That man could not be excommunicated because he was not a believer. The pope forgave him on his hospital bed and later visited him in jail.

On May 12, 1982, a Spanish priest assaulted the pope while the pope was visiting the shrine of Our Lady of Fatima in Portugal. With a raised bayonet, the priest was about to stab the pope in the back when the pope's bodyguard wrested him to the ground. The pope turned and blessed him unaware of the assault. This priest could have been excommunicated, but instead he served a six-year prison sentence and was expelled from Portugal afterwards.

Selling, making or distributing false relics also calls for excommunication. Any part of the bodily remains of a saint is designated as a sacred relic and so are the true cross of Jesus and His burial clothes, the shroud. The Early Church gathered the bones of the martyrs and placed them in a secure place. The faithful would come and venerate the martyrs' remains and many would be healed. Relics are not to be worshipped. Nothing could be more ridiculous than a dead man's bones to be instrumental in someone's healing. Nonetheless, the use of the bones of Elisha brought a dead man to life.
> Once while some Israelites were burying a man, suddenly they saw a band of raiders; so they threw the man's body into Elisha's tomb. When the body touched Elisha's bones, the man came to life and stood up on his feet" (2 Kings 13:21 NIV).

That is a remarkable miracle performed by God through contact with the relics of a saint.

Relics are sacramentals. Sacramentals are either objects or actions by which a person may receive a natural or spiritual favor from God. Sacramentals are widely used by all Christians. They use water, oil, wine, the laying on of hands, spoken words, etc.. The apostle Paul used handkerchiefs, aprons and even his shadow. Jesus used, among other things, mud and spittle.

> Having said this, he spit on the ground, made some mud with the saliva, and put it on the man's eyes. Go, he told him, wash in the Pool of Siloam (this word means Sent). So the man went and washed, and came home seeing (John 9:6–7 NIV).

God made matter, He loves matter, and He became matter Himself to accomplish our redemption. He uses sacramentals, matter to bestow grace upon us—an outer sign to effect an inner grace, spiritual or even natural. Grace is of many kinds, defined according to its creation and effects. Grace is an influence of God, operating in man to give life, to restore life, to strengthen life. It is a gift. There is nothing magical about it. It is just the way God operates in people's lives. Remember God uses the foolish things of this world to confound the wise.

Infallibility

Infallibility is not based on the pope being infallible, but on the infallibility of the Holy Spirit. As the Scriptures were inspired by the Holy Spirit and therefore constitute the truth, so is the proclamation of the Scriptures (doctrine and moral) by the pope, in conjunction with the bishops, infallible. It is the action of the Holy Spirit who conserves. The pope's personal views, his way of living, his shortcomings and sins have nothing to do with infallibility. There is no guarantee that a pope will not sin nor give a bad example.

Together the pope and the bishops form the teaching authority of the church, which is called the magisterium (from the Latin 'teaching'). The magisterium, guided and protected from error by the Holy Spirit, gives us certainty in matters of doctrine. The church is the custodian of the Bible and faithfully and accurately proclaims its message, a task that God has empowered it to do.

The magisterium is infallible when it teaches officially because Jesus promised to send the Holy Spirit to guide the apostles and their successors into all truth. "But when he, the Spirit of truth, comes, he will guide you into all truth" (John 16:13 NIV).

Only when the pope speaks from the chair of Peter does he speaks with the fullness of his authority as the successor of Peter. It is a metaphor that refers to the pope's authority to teach, not to where he sits when he teaches. From the chair of Peter is referred to as ex cathedra, meaning seat from the Latin *cathedra*. That is not an invention of the Catholic Church but from Jesus Himself.

> Then Jesus said to the crowds and to his disciples: "The teachers of the law and the Pharisees sit in Moses' seat. So you must obey them and do everything they tell you. But do not do what they do, for they do not practice what they preach" (Matthew 23:1–3 NIV).

Infallibility was always present in the Church since apostolic times. It is a doctrine that was implicit in the Early Church. Vatican I defined the doctrine of infallibility on July 18, 1870. Infallibility does not extend to proclamations of discipline, church policies and by no means includes impeccability of the pope or inerrancies in his private opinions. Christ's doctrine must and will be handed on by an infallible church guided by the Holy Spirit. Vatican II continued to state that the pope proclaims, by a definitive act, doctrines of faith or morals. Individual bishops do not enjoy the prerogative of infallibility. They can nevertheless proclaim Christ's doctrine infallible, and so can any believer when guided by the Holy Spirit.

An infallible pronouncement is usually made only when some doctrine has been called into question. Infallibility applies only to solemn, official teaching on faith and morals, not to disciplinary decisions or even unofficial comments on faith and morals. Infallibility is not a substitute for theological study on the part of the pope. What infallibility does do is prevent a pope from teaching as truth something that is in fact error. It does not help him know what is truth. He has to learn the truth the way we all do, through study. It is the Holy Spirit who prevents a pope from officially teaching error. Your close relationship with the Holy Spirit will also prevent you from being deceived and falling into error.

4. Why Choose Christianity in the First Place?

There are many belief systems and surely one can find one that suits one's taste. Then why bother with Christianity? The answer lies in our human nature. Every human being needs to be a Christian. It is a matter of life and death.

The Creation of Humankind

God is perfect. One of the facets of that perfection is giving and sharing. For God, that means sharing His life and His glory with others. Those others are His creation, all human beings. "Be perfect, therefore, as your heavenly Father is perfect" (Matthew 5:48 NIV).

"Jesus answered, 'If you want to be perfect, go, sell your possessions and give to the poor, and you will have treasures in heaven. Then come and follow me'" (Matthew 19:21 NIV). To be perfect is just part of the love that God has for us and the love that we must have for Him and others. Out of that love, God created men and women.

"The Lord God formed the man from the dust of the ground and breathed into his nostrils the breath of life, and the man became a living being" (Genesis 2:7 NIV). When God breathed on Adam, Adam's spirit was created, and that spirit united with the physical body and the physical mind. It resulted in a living human being. Adam was made from the dust of the ground and born of God in an instant. His body was alive, and his spirit was alive in the true sense. Man's spirit, mind and body were totally impregnated with God's life, thus becoming a living being in God's eye.

> So the Lord God caused the man to fall into a deep sleep; and while he was sleeping, he took one of the man's ribs and closed up the place with flesh. Then the Lord God made a woman from the rib he had taken out of the man, and he brought her to the man (Genesis 2:21–22 NIV).

The creation of Adam and Eve came about as the Bible tells us, pure and simple.

Characteristics of the Original Spirit, Mind and Body

1) They were made in the image and likeness of God, created in a higher class than angels or any other creature—perfect, whole and mature in spirit, mind and body. "Do you not know that we will judge angels?"(1 Corinthians 6:3 NIV).

   "Are not all angels ministering spirits sent to serve those who will inherit salvation?" (Hebrews 1:14 NIV).

2) The spirit was made out of the very essence of God, the mind and body were made from the dust of the ground.

3) The spirit was born of God with God's very life in him and her, the dwelling place of God Almighty. The mind and body enjoyed divine health and beauty. Beauty and health is part of God Himself. Since mankind was created in the image and likeness of God, it is understood that those attributes were part of Adam and Eve.

4) The spirit, mind and body were immortal and eternal. The original immortality was conditional to Adam's obedience to God. "And the Lord God commanded the man, 'You are free to eat from any tree in the garden; but you must not eat from the tree of knowledge of good and evil, for when you eat of it you will surely die'" (Genesis 2:16–17 NIV).

5) The spirit had the ability to make free choices and to make personal decisions; a totally free will. The mind and body were able to choose and to do freely whatever their desires were, including to eat or not to eat from the tree of knowledge of good and evil. The conscience gave clear guidance.

6) The spirit, mind and body had total and complete dominion and authority on and over the whole earth. "…let them rule over the fish of the sea and the birds of the air, over the livestock, over all the earth, and over all the creatures that move along the ground" (Genesis 1:26 NIV).

7) The spirit, mind and body were not affected by time or space.

8)   The spirit, mind and body operated in perfect faith. The heart (not the physical
     heart but the heart as part of the spirit) and mind were one—single minded.

9)   They walked in the spirit, in perfect love and fellowship with God.

10) In everything, they were blessed and not cursed. "God blessed them" (Genesis
     1:28 NIV).

The Bible does not tell us how long Adam and Eve lived the perfect life in the
Garden of Eden. They were not subjected to sickness or disease, but pain, as a
protective measure, was part of that perfect life. "To the woman he said, "I will
greatly increase your pains in childbearing" (Genesis 3:16 NIV). For pain to be
increased, it had to be there in the first place. But when Adam and Eve disobeyed
God, they suffered the consequences and their perfect life came to an end.

The Fall of Humankind

> Now the serpent was more crafty than any of the wild animals
> the Lord God had made. He said to the woman, "Did God really
> say, 'You must not eat from any tree in the garden'?"
> The woman said to the serpent, "We may eat fruit from the
> trees in the garden, but God did say, 'You must not eat fruit from
> the tree that is in the middle of the garden, and you must not touch
> it, or you will die.'"
> "You will not surely die," the serpent said to the woman. "For
> God knows that when you eat of it your eyes will be opened, and
> you will be like God, knowing good and evil."
> When the woman saw that the fruit of the tree was good for
> food and pleasing to the eye, and also desirable for gaining wisdom,
> she took some and ate it. She also gave some to her husband, who
> was with her, and he ate it. Then the eyes of both were opened, and
> they realized they were naked; so they sewed fig leaves together and
> made coverings for themselves (Genesis 3:1–7 NIV).

We do not know how long Adam and Eve lived the perfect life before they were
deceived by the craftiness of Satan, but the moment they disobeyed, disaster struck.
Instantly they died spiritually, God's life was no longer in them. Fear entered their
hearts for the first time. No longer did they operate in faith, but in fear—Satan's

mode of operation. Their spirit was still made out of the essence of God, but was deprived of God's life. In God's eye that is death. From that point, all Adam's offspring would be born of the flesh and not born of God. Every offspring would be born with a dead spirit, a spiritual stillbirth. But the damage did not stop there. Satan was cursed, Eve was cursed, Adam was cursed, all their offspring were cursed and the earth was cursed.

Who is Satan? To answer that question one has to go back in history. Satan is one of the three known archangels. Archangels are the chiefs, the leaders and rulers. We know three of them: Michael, Gabriel and Lucifer (Satan).

Lucifer, an archangel full of wisdom and of perfect beauty, who was anointed leader of worship, ruled over the earth as well as the heavenly powers and the demons. Jealousy, pride and rebellion entered his heart, and he said,

> I will ascend into heaven; I will exalt my throne above the stars of
> God; I will sit upon the mount of the congregate; I will ascend above
> the height of the clouds; I will be like the Most High (Isaiah 14:13–14
> NIV paraphrased).

The result was disastrous. Lucifer was cast out from the third heaven to the second heaven. He does not live on the earth, but he visits a lot. He rules from his place of authority. The heavenly powers that rebelled with him (one third of the angels) fell with him. Although Lucifer was hurled to the earth and expelled from the third heaven, he was not banished from the second heaven: his place of authority. Daniel describes heavenly warfare, and in Ephesians we see spiritual forces of evil in action in heavenly realms.

> But the prince of the Persian kingdom resisted me twenty-one days.
> Then Michael, one of the chief princes, came to help me, because I
> was detained there with the king of Persia (Daniel 10:13 NIV).

> For our struggle is not against flesh and blood, but against the
> rulers, against the authorities, against the powers of this dark world
> and against the spiritual forces of evil in the heavenly realms
> (Ephesians 6:12 NIV).

"How you have fallen from heaven, O morning star, son of the dawn! You have been cast to the earth, you who once laid low the nations!" (Isaiah 14:12 NIV). At his fall, the original earth, once ruled by Lucifer, experienced the fall and ruin and was destroyed because of his rebellion. Lucifer's nature changed. He became the father of liars and of murderers; a thief, a robber and a killer; deceitful, cruel, fierce and cunning.

The demons were a pre-Adamic race that lived on the earth. God had created them as spirits with bodies. The demons became disembodied spirits. They like to live in a body and may possess unbelievers and oppress believers. God never created an evil spirit. The demons became evil, disembodied spirits by their own choice. They were part of the nations laid low by Lucifer.

When Lucifer rebelled against God, he lost dominion over the earth. God's masterpieces, Adam and Eve, had perfect dominion over all the earth, but a jealous adversary, Lucifer, tricked them into disobeying God. At that point, Lucifer regained the dominion and authority he previously had on earth.

Everybody will be tempted here on earth, and Jesus was no exception. As a young man, Jesus was led by the Holy Spirit into the desert, where for forty days He was tempted by the devil.

> The devil led Him up to a high place and showed Him in an instant all the kingdoms of the world. And he said to Him, "I will give you all their authority and splendor, for it has been given to me, and I can give it to anyone I want to. So if you worship me, it will all be yours."
>
> Jesus answered, "It is written: Worship the Lord your God and serve Him only" (Luke 4:5–8 NIV).

The devil could talk like that, because Adam had lost all authority to Satan in the Garden of Eden more than four thousand years earlier. That situation changed drastically at the death and the resurrection of Jesus Christ. This is what Jesus said after the resurrection, "All authority in heaven and on earth has been given to me" (Matthew 28:18 NIV). That same authority is given by Jesus Christ to every believer.

Satan is waging a reign of terror upon the inhabitants of the earth. This will greatly intensify in the last days, especially during the Tribulation period. Nevertheless, he is doomed to defeat.

> And I saw an angel coming down out of heaven, having the key to the Abyss and holding in his hand a great chain. He seized the

dragon, that ancient serpent, who is the devil, or Satan, and bound him for a thousand years. He threw him into the Abyss, and locked and sealed it over him, to keep him from deceiving the nations anymore until the thousand years were ended. After that, he must be set free for a short time (Revelation 20:1–3 NIV).

When the thousand years are over, Satan will be released from his prison and will go out to deceive the nations in the four corners of the earth—Gog and Magog—to gather them for battle. In numbers they are like the sand on the seashore. They marched across the breadth of the earth and surrounded the camp of God's people, the city he loves. But fire came down from heaven and devoured them. And the devil, who deceived them, was thrown into the lake of burning sulfur, where the beast and the false prophet had been thrown. They will be tormented day and night for ever and ever (Revelation 20:7–10 NIV).

What is the final outcome of Adam and Eve's offspring? The next paragraph shows us specifically the damage done to God's greatest creation: the human beings.

Characteristics of the Fallen Spirit, Mind and Body

1) They no longer display the image and likeness of God. That image and likeness is tarnished and destroyed. "And just as we have borne the likeness of the earthly man [fallen Adam], so shall we bear the likeness of the man from heaven [the last Adam, Jesus Christ]" (1 Corinthians 15:49 NIV).

2) The spirit is still made out of the very essence of God; the mind and body of Adam's offspring are born of corrupt flesh. "Flesh gives birth to flesh, but the Spirit gives birth to spirit" (John 3:6 NIV).

3) The spirit is no longer born of God, but born of flesh. God's life is no longer in him or her. The dwelling place of God is destroyed. The mind and body are subject to sickness and disease.

4) The spirit is dead, eternally. The mind and body age, and death is the final outcome. In the Garden of Eden, God prevented Adam and Eve from eating from the tree of life lest they would never die. Their life span was set at about

one thousand years. That life span was further reduced to about one hundred and twenty years at the time of Noah's flood, because of the wickedness and iniquity of the people in those days. "Then the Lord said, 'My Spirit will not contend with man forever, for he is mortal, his days will be a hundred and twenty years'"(Genesis 6:3 NIV).

5) The free will of the spirit and the mind is greatly hampered by evil influences. The body often dictates the course of action that a person takes. The conscience is defiled and polluted. The will is obscured and weak. "They are darkened in their understanding and separated from the life of God because of the ignorance that is in them due to the hardening of their hearts" (Ephesians 4:18 NIV).

6) The spirit, mind and body have lost dominion and authority over the earth and the creatures of the earth. Satan regained that authority. "And he said to him, 'I will give you all their authority and splendor, for it has been given to me, and I can give it to anyone I want to'" (Luke 4:6 NIV).

7) The spirit, along with mind and body, is held captive by time and space. Acts gives us a good example of when the captivity of time and space is suspended for the mind and body.

> When they came up out of the water, the Spirit of the Lord suddenly took Philip away, and the eunuch did not see him again, but went on his way rejoicing. Philip, however, appeared at Azotus and traveled about, preaching the gospel in all the towns until he reached Caesarea (Acts 8:39–40 NIV).

8) The spirit, mind and body no longer operate in faith, but in fear. The triune human being is divided. "He answered, 'I heard you in the garden, and I was afraid because I was naked; so I hid'" (Genesis 3:10 NIV).

9) They walk in the flesh. The loving relationship and fellowship with God no longer exist.

10) They are cursed in everything. They are cursed in their spirits, minds and bodies. They are cursed in what they do, their work, their relationships, their finances and their surroundings. Natural disasters are part of the original curse. It is not God's doing, nevertheless many people blame God for it.

To the woman he said, "I will greatly increase your pain in childbearing; with pain you will give birth to children. Your desire will be for your husband, and he will rule over you."

To Adam he said, "Because you listened to your wife and ate from the tree about which I commanded you, 'You must not eat from it,'

Cursed is the ground because of you; through painful toil you will eat of it all the days of your life. It will produce thorns and thistles for you, and you will eat the plants of the field. By the sweat of your brow you will eat your food until you return to the ground" (Genesis 3:16–19 NIV).

The fall of man embodies a curse and a promise. "The seed of the woman" (Genesis 3:15 NIV) will redeem fallen man from the curse.

But it was not until about four thousand years later that the Son of God, Jesus Christ, came to redeem mankind. God needed a structure, an evolved civilization, a people to implement His plan of salvation. God was ready any time, but not His people. Even when He came, many did not receive Him. "He was in the world, and though the world was made through him, the world did not recognize him. He came to that which was his own, but his own did not receive him (John 1:10–11 NIV). But for all who receive and accept Him and still do, restoration is at hand.

The Restoration of Humankind

At the most tragic time in history for humankind, the fall of Adam and Eve, God had a plan to save all humankind. He made the promise, which came to pass about four thousand years later, with the first coming of Jesus Christ, His Son.

God came to humankind's rescue, as He had promised Adam. God cannot, as such, redeem humankind. There had to be a perfect man who could take Adam's place. Around the year A.D. 1, God the Father sent His Son Jesus to earth. God became like you and me. He was stripped of all godly attributes while on earth. Since He was not an offspring of Adam, He was spiritually alive and became the perfect ransom for all humankind. "And he is the head of the body, the church; he is the beginning and the firstborn from among the dead, so that in everything he might have supremacy" (Colossians 1:18 NIV).

"For what the law was powerless to do in that it was weakened by the sinful nature, God did by sending his own Son in the likeness of sinful man to be a sin offering" (Romans 8:3 NIV).

> Who being in very nature God, did not consider equality with God something to be grasped, but made himself nothing, taking the very nature of a servant, being made in human likeness. And being found in appearance as a man, he humbled himself and became obedient to death—even death on a cross! (Philippians 2:6–8 NIV).

In the year A.D. 33, Jesus gave His life for you and me so that we may live. He died by crucifixion. "God made Him who had no sin to be sin for us, so that in him we might become the righteousness of God" (2 Corinthians 5:21 NIV). All hell rejoiced. You see, the devil is not omniscient. He thought that was the end of the Son of God. The devil and the demons' triumph was very short lived. On the third day, Jesus rose from death by the power of the Holy Spirit. "And if the Spirit of him who raised Jesus from the dead is living in you, he who raised Christ from the dead will also give life to your mortal bodies through his Spirit, who lives in you" (Romans 8:11 NIV).

By His blood, death and resurrection, Jesus Christ restored humankind. Darkness changed to light, death to life, hate to love, chains to freedom and despair to joy. He redeemed us from the curse of eternal death, from sickness and disease, and from poverty and bondage. We have the privilege to become sons and daughters of God the Father and brothers and sisters of Jesus Christ. As such we are joint heirs with Jesus Christ.

So why choose Christianity in the first place? Because there is no other faith or religion that can give any human being life of the spirit, mind and body and make us immortal and eternal according to God. "...that everyone who believes in him may have eternal life" (John 3:15 NIV).

"I give them eternal life, and they shall never perish; no one can snatch them out of my hand" (John 10:28 NIV). "For the wages of sin is death, but the gift of God is eternal life in Christ Jesus our Lord" (Romans 6:23 NIV).

"And this is the testimony: God has given us eternal life, and this life is in his Son. He who has the Son has life; he who does not have the Son of God does not have life" (1 John 5:11–12 NIV).

There is no other faith or religion that can give birth to any human being to become a child, a son or a daughter, of God Almighty. "How great is the love the Father has lavished on us, that we should be called children of God! And that is what we are!" (1 John 3:1–2 NIV).

"I will be a Father to you, and you will be my sons and daughters, says the Lord Almighty" (2 Corinthians 6:18 NIV).

There is no other faith or religion that makes any human being a brother and a joint heir with Jesus Christ. "Now if we are children, then we are heirs—heirs of God and co-heirs with Christ, if indeed we share in his sufferings in order that we may also share in his glory" (Romans 8:17 NIV).

There is no other faith or religion that can give any human being spiritual power. Spiritual power is released in our lives, able to transform us and those around us.

- The power of God's forgiveness that sets us free.
- The power that enables us to forgive those who have hurt us.
- The power to resist what we know is wrong.
- The power of God's love, which fills us with love for Him and for others.
- The power of God's Spirit, which brings us the new life of Jesus.
- The power to get wealth to be able to help others and to implement the kingdom of God here on earth. "His divine power has given us everything we need for life" (2 Peter1:3 NIV).

There is absolutely no substitute for Christianity.

5. The Working of God the Father, God the Son and God the Holy Spirit among the People

Regardless of the affiliation of your denomination or lack of it, God works the same way among His people. He does not work in a certain way among the Catholics, in a different way among the Orthodox and still in an other way among the Protestants. No, God is neither swayed, nor influenced by our doctrine, but by the love we have for Him and His people. That is not to say He does not care about doctrine. Doctrine is the basic truth of the Christian belief system, the Christian faith based on the Scriptures, the Word of God. In fact, there should be no doctrinal differences within the Christian family. The differences stem from a misinterpretation of scriptural truths caused by ignorance and a refusal of the church leaders in charge to be guided and taught by the Holy Spirit. Often it is a rebellion to submit to a higher authority.

Doctrine was important to Jesus. He called an expert of that time to be His man of doctrine. It was Paul the Apostle. Paul had trouble with the other apostles, for them to accept the doctrine he was teaching. At times it took an intervention of God to change their mindset.

> When Peter came to Antioch, I opposed him to his face, because he was in the wrong. Before certain men came from James, he used to eat with the Gentiles. But when they arrived, he began to draw back and separate himself from the Gentiles because he was afraid of those who belonged to the circumcision group. The other Jews joined him in his hypocrisy, so that by their hypocrisy even Barnabas was led astray (Galatians 2:11–13 NIV).

God had to show Peter, through a vision, not to call anything impure that God has made clean.

> He said to them: You are well aware that it is against our law for a Jew to associate with a Gentile or visit him. But God has shown me that I should not call any man impure or unclean (Acts 10:28 NIV).

Revelation ends with a stern warning to anyone who adds or omits anything contained in that book.

> Anyone who breaks one of the least of these commandments and teaches others to do the same will be called least in the kingdom of

heaven, but whoever practices and teaches these commands will be
called great in the kingdom of heaven (Matthew 5:19 NIV).

Both references show clearly how important true doctrine is to God, and we the believers should do everything in our ability to make sure we proclaim and live by the truth.

The creed is the minimal doctrine required by every Christian. That is not to say everything else is superfluous. Jesus Christ is the author and perfecter of our faith, our belief system. Clearly there is a progression, a maturational process involved. An open mind and heart are needed to make changes and to accept the truth as the Holy Spirit reveals it to us. There should never be a division caused by doctrinal arguments or differences. God's doctrine is a doctrine of love. We should be known to the world by the love we have for each other and for our enemies. Love must become our nature, our character. "Everyone who loves has been born of God and knows God" (1 John 4:7 NIV). It could not be clearer than that.

We will be judged by our good works, deeds and works of love, and the love we have for Him and for one another. "In the same way, let your light shine before men, that they may see your good deeds and praise your Father in heaven" (Matthew 5:16 NIV).

"I ask that we love one another. And this is love: that we walk in obedience to His commands. As you have heard from the beginning, his command is that you walk in love" (2 John: 5–6 NIV). God has given us a doctrine of love and not of legalism. There is no excuse for having different doctrines in the body of Christ. The problem is not having disagreements but being unwilling to solve those disagreements in the light of the scriptural truths. The Early Church at the Council at Jerusalem had to solve some tough issues concerning Jewish/Gentile relations. It is related in Acts 15.

The Nicene Creed

Nowadays, the Nicene Creed (A.D. 325) is used as a profession of faith.

> We believe in one God the Father, the Almighty, maker of heaven
> and earth, of all that is seen and unseen.
> We believe in one Lord, Jesus Christ, the only Son of God, eternally
> begotten of the Father, God from God, Light from Light, true God
> from true God, begotten not made, one in being with the Father.
> Through him all things were made. For us men and for our salvation

he came down from heaven: by the power of the Holy Spirit he was born of the Virgin Mary, and became man. For our sake he was crucified under Pontius Pilate; he suffered, died and was buried. On the third day he rose again in fulfillment of the Scriptures; he ascended into heaven and is seated at the right hand of the Father.
He will come again in glory to judge the living and the dead.
And his kingdom will have no end.
We believe in the Holy Spirit, the Lord, the giver of life,
Who proceeds from the Father and the Son.
With the Father and the Son he is worshiped and glorified.
He has spoken through the prophets.
We believe in one holy catholic and apostolic Church.
We acknowledge one baptism for the forgiveness of sins.
We look for the resurrection of the dead, and the life of the world to come.
Amen (Nicene Creed, as cited in Broderick, 1987).

There are mostly three of these creedal doctrines that are questioned or denied as truth by some of the Christian denominations. They are the Holy Spirit, one holy catholic and apostolic church and Virgin Mary.

The Holy Spirit

The Holy Spirit is a real person; He is the third person of the Trinity. Third does not mean less, but He is equal to the Father and to the Son. Some regard Him as an it or a ghost or some kind of power. The truth about the Holy Spirit is basic doctrine, and anyone who does not believe that doctrine is not part of the Christian family. Refer to pages 153 and 154 for more information about Him.

The One, Holy, Catholic and Apostolic Church

The Protestants like to give catholic a different meaning, universal, that has nothing to do with the Roman Catholic Church. The church meaning in the creed has nothing to do with a denominational church but as the church Jesus Christ instituted. Catholic means true church. Refer back to page 22 for additional information.

The Marian Question

The Marian doctrine is one where Protestants and Catholics clash. It is a doctrine most bothersome to Protestants, who believe that Catholics worship Mary the Mother of God. Nothing could be further from the truth. Catholics venerate and honor Mary, an honor due to her. For almost two thousand years people have looked to Mary for answers to their troubles.

The account of the first miracle of Jesus is quite an eye opener.

> When the wine was all gone, Jesus' mother said to him: "They have no more wine."
>
> "Dear woman, why do you involve me?' Jesus replied. "My time has not yet come."
>
> His mother said to the servants, "Do whatever he tells you"

(John 2:3–5 NIV).

It was not God's timing, His time had not yet come. Mary ignored His remark; she wanted Him to do something about it. She cared for the bride and groom. She did not want them to be put to shame for not having enough wine. Jesus gave in to Mary's wish, even though His time had not yet come. He changed the water to wine. Every day Jesus will change your water to wine on the request of His mother whom He dearly loves. He will change your problems to victories, your sickness to health—spirit, mind and body. If you honor and venerate His mother, she will intercede for you at her Son's throne.

Lourdes in France and Fatima in Portugal are two famous locations where pilgrims from all over the world converge to seek favors from Mary. I personally, at the age of sixteen, went to Lourdes and saw firsthand the tremendous grace (divine influence) bestowed upon the believing pilgrims. Jesus uses His beloved mother as a channel to grant healing to His people. Pope John Paul II attributed the failed assassination attempt years ago to the protection of the Virgin Mary, of whom he was a staunch venerator and promoter. How many people have missed their blessing and healing by ignoring the way God works? One of these ways is going through Mary instead of going to Jesus directly. Embrace it whole-heartedly and be made whole.

Jesus was formed in Mary's womb by the power of the Holy Spirit. Jesus Christ must also be formed in us by the power of the Holy Spirit. We must decline, and He must increase. We must take on the nature and character of Jesus Christ, He in us and we in Him. Jesus is the firstborn of many, the Christ generation. Mary is the spiritual mother of many; she is the new Eve, with Jesus Christ being the firstborn.

Until recently it was believed that the blood of a child came solely from the father. Scientific proof reveals otherwise: it comes from the father and the mother. Mary had to be sinless, not touched by the original sin, to produce a child without polluted blood in him. It is what the Roman Catholic Church calls' the Immaculate Conception', a thorn in the flesh for Protestants. The term does not refer to Christ's conception in Mary's womb without the intervention of a human father, that is the Virgin Birth. Mary was not conceived by the power of the Holy Spirit; she was conceived by the normal way but was conceived without the original sin and its stain. The essence of original sin consists in the deprivation of sanctifying grace, and its stain is a corrupt nature. Mary was preserved from these defects by God's grace; from the first instant of her existence, she was in the state of sanctifying grace (made holy by divine influence, original sin did not touch her) and was free from the corrupt nature original sin brings.

"The angel Gabrielle said, 'Hail, full of grace, the Lord is with you'" (Luke 1:28 NIV paraphrased). Full of grace, full of divine influence is both intensive and extensive; it extended from the first moment of conception onward. Mary was in a state of sanctifying grace from the first moment of her existence. Mary needed a savior not to save her as He saved all of us but a savior to preserve her from the stain of original sin and its consequences. She was therefore redeemed by the grace of Christ, but in a special way—by anticipation.

"And Mary said: My soul glorifies the Lord and my spirit rejoices in God my Savior" (Luke 1:46–47 NIV). By receiving Christ's grace at her conception, she had His grace applied to her before she was touched by original sin and its stain. In other words, she was redeemed in a more exalted fashion, by reason of the merits of her Son. She has more reason to call God her Savior than we do, because He saved her in an even more glorious way. It is clear if Jesus would have been born of Mary, Mary not being conceived immaculate, Jesus would be touched by original sin, and His offspring the Christ generation, all born from above, would also be touched by original sin. Therefore there would be no redemption possible. Mary is the New Eve.

The doctrine of the Assumption declares that at the end of her life on earth Mary was assumed—body, mind and spirit—into heaven, just as Enoch and Elijah. Mary did not ascend into heaven like Jesus did. Christ by His own power, ascended into heaven. Mary was assumed or taken up to heaven by God. She did not do it under her own power. Whether Mary died or not does not impair the integrity of the doctrine of the Assumption.

If Enoch and Elijah and perhaps others were taken up into heaven—body, mind and spirit—why do Protestants fail to accept that Mary the Mother of Jesus Christ could have been assumed, taken up, too? After all, if Mary were immaculately conceived (and she was) then it would follow that she would not suffer the corruption of the grave, which is a consequence of sin.

Some Catholics believe Mary and Joseph never had sexual intercourse, and Jesus was their only child. The Scriptures are very clear about the subject. "But he had no union with her until she gave birth to a son" (Matthew 1:25 NIV). Joseph and Mary had no sexual intercourse until Jesus was born. True love, including sexual love among married couples, does not render vile but rather sanctify the spouses involved.

> "Where did this man get this wisdom and these miraculous powers?" they asked. "Isn't this the carpenter's son? Isn't his mother's name Mary, and aren't his brothers James, Joseph, Simon and Judas? Aren't all his sisters with us? Where did this man get all these things?" And they took offense at him (Matthew 13:54–57 NIV).

According to these Bible verses we know with certainty that Joseph and Mary had five boys: Jesus, James, Joseph, Simon and Judas and at least two daughters (his sisters plural). Even with these overwhelmingly convincing scriptures, some people still insist that Scriptures meant not blood brothers but His brethren.

The Christian Walk with God

In the Christian walk with God are two well-defined phases, and each contains different levels of maturity. A person cannot skip a phase or a level of a phase thinking he is doing all right. In the natural world, there are seven maturational levels. Some children, encouraged by their parents, skip a level here and there. The result is an underdeveloped person in those skipped areas. The following is a good illustration from a natural point of view of when crawling and creeping is partially skipped.

Crawling is done on the tummy, while creeping is done on hands and knees. At the beginning, children do not crawl in a cross pattern way but in a homolateral way. If a person walks in a homolateral way he or she is, to a certain degree, neurologically disorganized. Crawling is pure movement. There are three crawling modes:

1. Homologous: moving both arms together and moving both legs together.
2. Homolateral: moving the arm and the leg of one side together and then the arm and the leg of the other side.
3. Cross pattern: moving the left arm and the right leg together and the right arm and left leg together.

Cross pattern is the most efficient way of moving on the floor. Get rid of all restrictive devices, playpens, strollers and walkers. Better yet, save your money; do not buy them. Do not push the child; rather provide the proper stimulation. You cannot skip a level; it will cause a problem of disorganization in the central nervous system. Sitting prematurely may cause more problems; babies do not have the muscles to support the spine. Walking prematurely often causes those children never to walk a good walk. Crawling and creeping is of the utmost importance in proper development of the brain. To deprive whole generations of children the opportunity to do so, will result in a low level of intelligence in that society: neurologically disorganized and inefficient. The tribes in the Amazon are a good example: no written language and poor conceptional skills. According to researchers at the Institutes for the Achievement of Human Potential, located in Philadelphia, Pennsylvania, it is a proven fact that teenagers with poor reading skills, who did not crawl and creep enough while a baby, will only improve drastically by crawling and creeping.

Most learning disabilities stem from the pons and mid-brain areas. Creeping is very important to organize the brain. You cannot go to walking unless you have mastered the crawling and creeping. Walking does not organize the same brain area as does crawling and creeping. The medulla is in control of reflex functions, the pons is responsible for vital functions and the mid-brain is responsible for meaningful functions. Dress your child in socks and long pants for creeping. Jogging develops your respiration and so does creeping develop your child's respiration.

Changing from a quadruped to an upright position will free your child's hands. Do not hold your child's hands. The balance mechanism (the vestibular part of the brain) needs opportunity to learn how to balance for walking. Raising the child's hands to hold yours will throw the child off balance. In Western cultures, where babies are not given ample opportunities to crawl and creep, well-developed hip joints are less prominent than in cultures where babies do get those opportunities. Newborn babies do not yet have any hip sockets. When babies crawl flat on their bellies, with their legs flat on the floor, the head of the femur (upper leg bone) digs into the hipbone in a lateral way. When creeping, the head of the femur digs into the hipbone in a vertical direction. It becomes a universal joint, which permits the leg to move in many directions.

God's interaction with people depends on the individual's level of growth and maturity. Nobody in his right mind gives a toddler a loaded handgun, neither does your heavenly Father give a spiritual toddler some of His power, which is more powerful than an atomic bomb.

The two phases are the Love Your God Phase, developed through intrapersonal spiritual intelligence, and the Love Others Phase, developed through interpersonal spiritual intelligence. Intelligence here means ability of the spirit, the human spirit.

The Intrapersonal, Spiritual Intelligence

The intrapersonal, spiritual intelligence is who you are. It deals with the inner self: the spirit with the conscience and the heart. It is to know yourself: your body, your physical mind, your temperament, your spirit and your character. It is to be able to form an accurate, honest model of oneself, to see your true self with the strengths, the weaknesses, the faults and the good traits. It is to achieve a personal identity. There is nobody like you, so don't try to be somebody else. Unless you achieve that personal identity, your self-esteem will always be at the mercy of influences and circumstances. It is to be able to use that model to operate effectively in life. You can stand up to any attack, you yourself are a stronghold, and the challenges of life are unable to shake or defeat you in any way. It works from the outside in; body, mind and spirit. Without a personal relationship with God the Father, God the Son and God the Holy Spirit, no person will attain a truthful intrapersonal intelligence. God and His word are the revelators of your self. "Love the Lord your God with all your heart and with all your soul [mind] and with all your strength [body]" (Deuteronomy 6:5 NIV). This is the first and greatest commandment of God given to the human race. By activating this commandment, you will launch the intrapersonal intelligence in your life. It will be up to you how far you will go!

The Interpersonal, Spiritual Intelligence

The interpersonal, spiritual intelligence is what you do. It is the ability to know and to understand other people. This can only happen if you know and understand yourself (intrapersonal intelligence). It is the ability to interact effectively and cooperatively with others. "Love your neighbor as yourself" (Mark 12:31 NIV). This second commandment given by God to the human race makes that interaction cooperative, effective and possible. It works from the inside out; from the spirit, through the mind, by the body.

Function determines structure is a law that applies to the natural as well as the spiritual realm. Intelligence is a pure product of use. The more you make use of it, the better it becomes. All intelligence layers are subject to that law.

The Love Your God Phase

"Love the Lord your God with all your heart…" (Mark 12:30 NIV).

Before anyone can have a relationship with God that person must be born from above, born of God, born again in spirit, mind and body, not just spirit, but mind and body as well, a totally new creation. Refer to the section in Chapter 8 entitled, *How Do I Become Born of God?* When you were born of your earthly parents, that was not religion; your natural birth was not religion; growing up, maturing and being given authority and power was not religion. Then why do most people think the birth from above, growing up and maturing as a Christian is religion or being given power and authority and exercising that authority and power is religion? It is mind-boggling how so many people are deceived.

Without any works or merits of your own, but just by believing in Jesus Christ, accepting Him, and asking Him to come into your heart you became born of God, born again. It was His responsibility to come to you. Christ in you. The only limitation for Him is you. To remove that limitation, work is required by you. You are the only one who can remove any limitation, but you will need help, and that help must come from the Holy Spirit. Jesus, the Son of God, gave us the example of how to rely on the Holy Spirit.

Jesus, the Son of God, while walking here on earth, was totally perfect man, stripped of all godly attributes.

Who, being in very nature God, did not consider equality with God something to be grasped, but made himself nothing, taking the very nature of a servant, being made in human likeness. And being found in appearance as a man, he humbled himself and became obedient to death—even death on a cross!" (Philippians 2:6–8 NIV).

He could not perform any miracles except through the power of the Holy Spirit and He was completely and totally dependent on the Holy Spirit for His mission here on earth. Pause for a moment and think about it; how Jesus Himself had to rely constantly on the Holy Spirit. How much more must we, imperfect as we are and replacing Jesus here on earth, rely on the Holy Spirit.

The Gift of the Holy Spirit

The person must love Jesus. The proof of that love is obedience to what He commands.

"If you love me, you will obey what I command. And I will ask the Father, and he will give you another Counselor to be with you forever—the Spirit of truth" (John 14:15–17 NIV).

"We are witnesses of these things, and so is the Holy Spirit, whom God has given to those who obey Him" (Acts 5:32 NIV).

When the two conditions are fulfilled, nothing stands in the way for you to receive the Holy Spirit. All you have to do is ask your heavenly Father. The Holy Spirit is a gift.

"And you will receive the gift of the Holy Spirit. The promise is for you and your children and for all who are far off—for all whom the Lord our God will call" (Acts 2:38–39 NIV).

The giving of the Holy Spirit to a person is a sign of acceptance by God of that person. "God, who knows the heart, showed that he accepted them by giving the Holy Spirit to them, just as he did to us" (Acts 15:8 NIV).

"I [John the Baptist] baptize you with water, but He [Jesus] will baptize you with the Holy Spirit" (Mark 1:8 NIV).

It is Jesus who baptizes you with the Holy Spirit. You ask the Father, and then Jesus, through his established spiritual authority in your area or your surroundings, will, by the laying on of hands, baptize you with the Holy Spirit. That authority may be your local pastor, a visiting evangelist or any Spirit-filled believer. A believer who does not know the Holy Spirit cannot give what he himself does not have. God is not restricted in His ways as to how to give the Holy Spirit. "Then Peter and John placed their hands on them, and they received the Holy Spirit" (Acts 8:17 NIV).

At times blowing or breathing on a person has the same results. "Again Jesus said, 'Peace be with you! As the Father has sent me, I am sending you.' And with that he breathed on them and said, 'Receive the Holy Spirit'" (John 20:21–22 NIV).

To baptize means to dip, to plunge or to immerse. In regards to baptizing with the Holy Spirit it means to pour out or to pour over. So the Holy Spirit is poured on or poured over a person.

Dying to Oneself

Before anything substantial can happen in your walk with God, you must die to yourself; you must decrease and Jesus must increase. The conditions for dying to yourself are summed up in three words: yield, submit and surrender, in that order. They are synonyms with a difference.

First you yield your body to the Holy Spirit. Yielding means giving way with an implication of compliance. You do not yield to temptation, but you yield to the Holy Spirit. The desires of your physical body do not control you anymore, but you control them. You must "offer your bodies as living sacrifices, holy and pleasing to God" (Romans 12:1 NIV).

You must submit your mind to the Holy Spirit. Submitting means giving up all resistance and giving in to the power, the will or authority of another.

"Do not conform any longer to the pattern of this world, but be transformed by the renewing of your mind" (Romans 12:2 NIV). You renew your mind so that it conforms to the Word of God and to the influence of the Holy Spirit. You stay in control of your decisions and your choices.

"The seventy-two returned with joy and said, 'Lord, even the demons submit to us in your name'" (Luke 10:17 NIV). Demons never surrender to anybody.

"…the sinful mind is hostile to God. It does not submit to God's law, nor can it do so" (Romans 8:7 NIV).

"Now as the church submits to Christ [not surrender], so also wives should submit to their husbands in everything" (Ephesians 5:24 NIV). God does not delight in a surrendered church but a submitted church. Many husbands confuse submit with surrender and force their will down the throat of their wives, and they have the gall to use God's Word to back up their demands.

"Submit yourselves, then, to God. Resist the devil, and he will flee from you" (James 4:7 NIV). Again this verse emphasizes submit and not surrender.

You must surrender your spirit to the Holy Spirit. Surrendering means giving up control or possession and is always preceded by a struggle, a resistance or a fight. Your spirit is the real you. Before you are able to surrender you must first die to yourself, not a physical death but a spiritual death. This spiritual death is not to be confused with the dead spirit of an unborn-again person. Dying to yourself does not come easily. Dying to yourself starts with your physical body; next is your mind and then your spirit.

"They are not of the world, even as I am not of it" (John 17:16 NIV).

"I have been crucified with Christ and I no longer live, but Christ lives in me" (Galatians 2:20 NIV).
First of all, after you have died to yourself, you are no longer of the world; you are crucified with Christ and no longer live, but Christ lives in you.

"And when Jesus had cried out again in a loud voice, he gave up [surrendered] his spirit" (Matthew 27:50 NIV).

"Jesus called out in a loud voice, 'Father, into your hands I commit [surrender] my spirit'" (Luke 23:46 NIV).

"They said to the Ammonites, 'Tomorrow we will surrender to you, and you can do to us whatever seems good to you'" (1 Samuel 11:10 NIV).

God looks for yielded vessels (bodies), submitted minds and surrendered spirits. God does not want your minds surrendered but submitted. He created you a free person; he is not glorified by zombies. Some people surrender their body, their mind and their spirit to the devil. They will be totally possessed by evil spirits. After they kill a person or persons or commit other gruesome atrocities, they say, "The devil made me do it." They forget that the devil has only as much power over them as they allow him to have.

We find a very good example of yielding, submitting and surrendering in Genesis 32:22–31 (NIV).

> That night Jacob got up and took his two wives, his two maidservants and his eleven sons and crossed the ford of the Jabbok. After he had sent them across the stream, he sent over all his possessions. So Jacob was left alone, and a man wrestled with him till daybreak. When the man saw that he could not overpower him, he touched the socket of Jacob's hip so that his hip was wrenched as he wrestled with the man. Then the man said, " Let me go, for it is daybreak."
>
> But Jacob replied, "I will not let you go unless you bless me."
>
> The man asked him, "What is your name?"
>
> "Jacob," he answered.
>
> Then the man said, " Your name will no longer be Jacob, but Israel, because you have struggled with God and with men and have overcome."
>
> Jacob said, " Please tell me your name."
>
> But he replied, " Why do you ask my name?" Then he blessed him there.
>
> So Jacob called the place Peniel, saying, "It is because I saw God face to face, and yet my life was spared."
>
> The sun rose above him as he passed Peniel, and he was limping because of his hip."

To die to yourself you have to get up and move from where you are to a new location. You unsettle yourself, the way you think, the way you do things. Jacob detached himself from his wives, his servants and his sons; the most precious persons in his life. Jesus says in Matthew 10:37 (NIV), "Anyone who loves his father or mother more than me is not worthy of me; anyone who loves his son or daughter more than me is not worthy of me."

Then Jacob detached himself from all material possessions. Material things will keep you bound and captive unless you release them to God. If they are your treasures, God cannot be part of you. "For where your treasure is, there your heart will be also" (Matthew 6:21 NIV). Jacob was left alone—no one and nothing stayed with him.

Dying to yourself, you must do it by yourself. It is a struggle between you and God. Without God, there will be no struggle, and there will be no dying either. It is a time of darkness, at least that's the way it is perceived by human nature. You struggle till you have victory over yourself, till daybreak. That daybreak may come in days, years or in a lifetime, it's up to you.

"When the man saw that he could not overpower him, he touched the socket of Jacob's hip so that his hip was wrenched as he wrestled with the man" (Genesis 32:25 NIV). At first this seems controversial, you may ask yourself why God Almighty could not overpower Jacob. Before Jacob was able to yield his body to God, God had to touch him. Only then was Jacob in a state to yield his body. The other noteworthy point is God does not go against your will; He will never overpower you. You must submit your mind to Him.

Our body and mind are not made perfect the minute we are born-again; a thorn in the flesh is given us, which stays with us as long as we live here on earth. To understand a thorn in the flesh, let's see what Paul the Apostle had to say about it.

> To keep me from becoming conceited because of these surpassingly great revelations, there was given me a thorn in my flesh, a messenger of Satan, to torment me. Three times I pleaded with the Lord to take it away from me. But He said to me, "My grace is sufficient for you, for my power is made perfect in weakness" (2 Corinthians 12:7–9 NIV).

A thorn in the flesh can be anything that is not perfect, not of God. It is the consequence of the fall of Adam and Eve: insults, hardships, persecutions, sickness, disease, difficulties, weaknesses, etc. They are all messengers of Satan. We can turn the thorns in the flesh into beautiful roses by dying to ourselves in yielding our body and submitting our mind to God. "I will not let you go unless you bless me" This speaks of a submitted mind, not a surrendered mind. Jacob let God touch him then hung onto God and request He bless him. And God blessed him. But not only that, He also changed him, from Jacob to Israel, from supplanter (Up to then he always took hold of the possessions of others: his brother's birthright, his father's blessings, his father-in-law's flocks and herds.) to Israel, prince with God.

It is so important to understand the difference between submitting and surrendering, yet most if not all dictionaries list them as synonyms. Here is a natural example: You see a dentist. You yield your body, more specifically your mouth and teeth to him. He suggests that you need a tooth pulled, you agree, you allow him to do it; you submit your will (mind) to him. Then he suggests he hypnotize you so you will feel no pain. You agree again; he hypnotizes you; you surrendered your will, your mind to him; he can do with you whatever he likes to do; you have no say in it anymore.

The only time a person should surrender to another person is among spouses. To reach total loving communion in the act of lovemaking, both husband and wife have to yield their bodies, submit their minds and surrender their spirits to each other. And they will be one in body, mind and spirit. Often only their bodies are yielded; no loving communion is taking place, no oneness and no likeness in the image of God.

Dying to yourself, yielding your body, submitting your mind and surrendering your spirit is not a one-time occurrence but a constant process and it produces the right priorities in your life.

Raising your arms and hands to the Lord is a physical sign of surrendering, an outward sign. You are in the most vulnerable position there is. This outward sign should be preceded by an inner yielding of your body, a submitting of your mind and a surrendering of your spirit. Some people criticize the falling under the power of God or the way it is produced or initiated like the laying on of hands, blowing on you, etc. We should not criticize the working of the Holy Spirit. The main thing is that a particular person is touched by God, healed in his or her physical body, restored, set free from any bondage, blessed with God's spiritual gifts but most of all blessed with God's presence and love.

While lying on the ground, under the power of God, you may experience all kinds of physical manifestations. Some people weep uncontrollably, others shake or feel a numbness but almost all the time you feel total peace, you are wrapped in a blanket of God's love and the warmth of God's presence surrounds you. I say 'God' because it could be Jesus, the Holy Spirit or the Father. Your spiritual senses are greatly sharpened; you see clearly; it makes it easier for you to see the truth and to live by the truth.

God may speak to you (your spirit) and give you specific instructions and guidelines: things you must change, people you must forgive or work He wants you to do. It is all part of your loving Father nurturing you, sustaining you and bringing you to maturity. How intense and rewarding your experience is, is up to you. It is your choice to bring to fulfillment what is imparted to you by the Most High.

The Holy Spirit Speaks to You. Are You Listening?

One thing is certain—the Holy Spirit speaks to us, but, unfortunately, we do not hear Him, or we hear Him seldom. The culprit is not the Holy Spirit; rather we are the ones who neglect to listen. He speaks to us in more than one way. We are spirits. As such He speaks to our spirits even though we may hear or perceive Him in the natural realm.

The Holy Spirit comes to us when we are quiet. That does not necessarily imply a quietness away from the world or an isolated place where you are totally alone and where complete absence of noise exists. These things may help but are not a prerequisite. I am talking about an inner quietness. You may be busy, noise may surround you, but you operate with an inner peace where your inner conversation is not overpowering the still small voice of the Holy Spirit. The Holy Spirit has twenty-four hours a day access to you to speak to you. Are you ready? We may not hear Him, and we may blame others for it, but mostly we are to be blamed for not listening and not hearing.

The Holy Spirit speaks to you in different ways. Most of the time it is through the Word of God. He will bring to remembrance a certain verse or paragraph and give you revelation through it. Other times, while you are reading the Bible, suddenly a verse jumps out at you and takes on a whole new meaning you never noticed before. Or the Holy Spirit speaks through the Word of God while a preacher or any person proclaims the Word.
He speaks to you through your conscience. Each time you come close to Him, or when you start praying, He reminds you of the thing or things in your life that are not right. He wants you to change them before you can have a loving relationship with Him.

He speaks to you, to your spirit, any time of the day or night, no matter in what situation you may find yourself.

"The Spirit told Philip, 'Go to that chariot and stay near it'" (Acts 8:29 NIV).

He speaks to you through a natural event or occurrence. At one time, I was thinking about a certain situation in my life, which was very bothersome, and wondering how to handle it. While thinking about it I zipped my jacket; at that very moment, the Holy Spirit spoke to my spirit, "Zip your mouth." It turned out to be the best advice.

He speaks to you through visions, which are mental images. People may talk to you in those visions. Visions happen while you are awake, not to be confused with hallucinations.

He speaks to you through other persons. Often those persons are not even aware that the Holy Spirit is ministering to you through them.

At times, He may use your mouth and tongue to speak to you audibly and loudly to get your attention quickly. You may be in the process of doing something very foolishly or bad and the Holy Spirit wants to prevent that, so He gets your attention immediately. "...for it will not be you speaking, but the Spirit of your Father speaking through you" (Matthew 10:20 NIV).

He may make use of an animal to speak to you. In the Old Testament the story of Balaam shows us the diversity by which the Holy Spirit speaks to us human beings. Obviously Balaam did not listen to God, so God used a donkey to get his attention. "Then the Lord opened the donkey's mouth, and she said to Balaam, 'What have I done to you to make you beat me these three times?'" (Numbers 22:28 NIV). Read the whole chapter; it will make you laugh; God has the greatest sense of humor. The closest I ever came to an event where an animal and the Holy Spirit were involved is the following true story, which happened in 1995. I was on my way to a certain address to do electrical work. No matter how hard I tried to find the place, I could not. I found the house with the number next to the number where I was supposed to work. So I decided to knock at that door and ask for it. The front yard was fenced in with a small door, leading straight to the house. I entered and closed the door behind me and walked towards the entrance. Three steps were leading to the house door, which was open. I was about to engage the first step when a fierce pit bull flew through the open door at me. There was no escape. I raised my arm to ward off the dog, but the next thing I noticed he was hanging with his clenched, strong jaws on my left wrist. Suddenly, I started barking fiercely at the wild animal. Stunned, he let go, looked at me in disbelief, turned around, tail between his legs and disappeared into the house. The owner came out, asked what I wanted, told me the neighbor was half a mile away because of the funny shape of the road. I did not tell him about the dog, in fact I was trespassing. What good would it have done? Under the influence of the Holy Spirit, my mouth was barking at the opportune time to save me from being torn into pieces. Even my wrist was unharmed—not even a scratch. The dog's teeth marks can still be seen today on my wristwatch's metal bracelet. Possibly, I was barking in a language understandable by the dog. There are situations where there is no time for the Holy Spirit to speak to you. He just will take over.

We, myself, my wife and my daughter, were driving in our family car to the local shopping mall. As usual, my wife prayed in tongues in the back seat. Out of the blue, the car in front of us stopped abruptly. At that very moment someone (the Holy Spirit) took over the steering wheel. For the next ten seconds that steering wheel turned rapidly several revolutions to the right then to the left and again to the right. I became the observer and not the doer. Miracle-like, the car fitted in an empty slot between the fast moving traffic in the other lane. I also noticed the horrified people on the sidewalk. They threw their arms up in the air, opened their mouths to scream, and then when nothing happened, closed their mouths again without uttering a single sound. Everything turned to normal again: no accident, no scratch and no sound, thanks to the Holy Spirit.

Often we do not hear the Holy Spirit, because our mind and body get in the way. So He uses times and methods when our mind and/or our body are out of order.

While we speak in tongues, the Holy Spirit speaks to our spirit. "This is what we speak, not in words taught us by human wisdom but in words taught by the Spirit, expressing spiritual truths in spiritual words" (1 Corinthians 2:13 NIV).

You may be slain in the Spirit. While you are slain in the Spirit you fall under the power of God. The power of God is so immense, no one can stand in His presence and survive unless God shields and protects him. God uses only as much power as is needed to overcome our resistance and to accomplish what He wants to accomplish. Many times, when God wants to heal you, to anoint you, to speak to you, to impart a spiritual gift to you, to bathe you in His presence, to love you and so forth or even to give you directions, He slays you: you fall under His power. You may find yourself in a charged atmosphere where God's presence is so thick, so rich and tangible, you just crumble and fall on the floor.

Often we put up resistance, our mind becomes a hindrance to what God wants to do. Falling under His power partly suspends our physical senses and bypasses our mind, so that God can easily act on our spirit. When you are slain in the Spirit your physical body and your mind are practically out of order, but your spirit becomes acutely aware and sensitive to the things of the spirit. You become numb to your surroundings, your physical senses are dulled but your spiritual senses are greatly sharpened.

Paul, the apostle, on his way to Damascus, fell under the power of God. "As he neared Damascus on his journey, suddenly a light from heaven flashed around him. He fell to the ground and heard a voice say to him, "Saul, Saul, why do you persecute me?" (Acts 9:3 NIV).

The Holy Spirit speaks to you through dreams while you are asleep. He wakes you up in the middle of the night, not fully, but just enough that your spirit is fully aware, but your mind and body are still drunk with sleep. Many times the Holy Spirit speaks to me just prior to waking up in the morning. In the minute timeframe between sleep and wakefulness, He is able to speak to me without me getting in His way.

Listening and hearing the Holy Spirit is not enough, you must respond to Him, and that response should always turn into action. Real communication is never a monologue.

Jesus Is Formed in Us by the Holy Spirit

It is the duty of the Holy Spirit to reveal Jesus Christ to us. He always points and guides us to Jesus. The Holy Spirit does not seek His own glory but the glory of Jesus. He is always in the background, in the shadow. He is self-effacing.

"He [the Holy Spirit] will bring glory to me [Jesus] by taking from what is mine and making it known to you" (John 16:14 NIV). When you live a lifetime with your spouse, both of you become alike; your tastes change, your thinking changes and your very being changes. Walking in the spirit and living with the Holy Spirit will change your life, and you become Christ-like; Jesus is formed in you.

"...The Holy Spirit will come upon you, and the power of the Most High will overshadow you" (Luke 1:35 NIV). As Jesus was conceived by the Holy Spirit in the womb of Mary, so will Jesus be formed in you by the Holy Spirit.

At that stage, what is required of you is the first command, "Love your God with all your heart [spirit], with all your mind and with all your might [body]" (Deuteronomy 6:5 NIV paraphrased).

The Holy Spirit is forming Jesus in you by the work He does on you, by dwelling within you and by fellowship and communion with you. He gives you life and freedom, transforms, renews, helps, leads, points out, confirms, shows, teaches, instructs, counsels, enlightens, reveals, gives understanding, dreams and visions, intercedes, searches, encourages, strengthens, predicts, warns, keeps you from harm, admonishes, compels, convicts, witnesses, testifies, determines, reminds, controls, distributes, cleanses with water and with fire, sanctifies and gives rest. You will grow and grow and grow, spiritually. God is not looking for ability but character; Christ-like character is built in you. You can then say with Paul the Apostle, "It is no longer I who lives but Christ lives in me" (Galatians 2:20 NIV paraphrased).

"I am the true vine, and my Father is the gardener. He cuts off every branch in me that bears no fruit, while every branch that does bear fruit he prunes so that it will be even more fruitful" (John 15:1–2 NIV).

Once Jesus is formed in you, you must remain in Him.
> I am the vine; you are the branches. If a man remains in me and I in him, he will bear much fruit; apart from me you can do nothing. If anyone does not remain in me, he is like a branch that is thrown away and withers; such branches are picked up, thrown into the fire and burned. If you remain in me and my words remain in you, ask whatever you wish, and it will be given you. This is to my Father's glory, that you bear much fruit, showing yourselves to be my disciples (John 15:5–8 NIV).

It is interesting to know how a real vine is pruned. Pruning a vine is a very appropriate picture to illustrate what happens in the spiritual realm when God the Father prunes your spirit. Three questions are important in pruning a vine: when, how and what.

When: The proper season as well as the proper weather temperature is vital. A vine cannot be pruned in the spring when the sap starts rising. Any cut at that time could be fatal to the vine. It could bleed to death. Similarly, a young believer is not pruned since it may destroy him or her. Long shoots are trimmed in the summer. These shoots do not bear any fruits. By trimming them it provides more nourishment to the fruit bearing branches. The bulk of the pruning is done late fall or early winter depending on weather temperatures. Too warm or freezing temperatures should be avoided. Freezing temperatures could kill the eyes or buds near the cut. Too warm temperatures may leave too much sap in the branch, freezing cold may then follow and freeze the eyes. After already bearing some spiritual fruit, the young believer is pruned. It does not come as too great a shock to him or her. He or she is able to withstand the pruning. Usually a period of spiritual rest follows.

What is cut and pruned determines how much fruit the branch will bear. Grape vines only bear grapes on the previous year's wood. In the fall, for instance, you trim back to two eyes the branch grown that year. In the spring, these two eyes or buds grow into a branch and it is on these branches that grapes appear. Spiritually, you bear fruit on this year's revelation based on last year's foundation.

How is the way you trim, cut and prune. The angle you cut the branch and also the distance from the eye where you cut are important. The Father's pruning is tailored to everybody's personality and need. No two persons are alike; hence no two persons are pruned alike.

It is obvious for any branch to bear fruit it must remain connected to the vine and connected to the other branches. How do we do that in the spiritual realm? We love Jesus and we love others.

Walking in the Spirit

Your spirit must be alive; you must be born-again to be able to walk in the spirit. An unbeliever always walks in the flesh, while a believer is capable but does not necessarily walk in the spirit. Walking in the spirit depends on the state of your spirit and of your mind; it will have a tremendous effect on your whole being: body, mind and spirit. You will operate and live in total liberty, freedom and love.
Walking in the spirit is walking with God. The greatest example of walking with God in the Scriptures is Enoch.

> When Enoch had lived 65 years, he became the father of
> Methuselah. And after he became the father of Methuselah, Enoch
> walked with God 300 years and had other sons and daughters.
> Altogether, Enoch lived 365 years. Enoch walked with God; then he
> was no more, because God took him away" (Genesis 5:21–24 NIV).

Scriptures do not tell a lot about Enoch. He did not die, and God took him at an early age away. In those days, reaching a thousand years was not uncommon. What a relationship between Enoch and God must have developed over the period of 300 years. So God simply took him away.

Two principles determine if you walk in the spirit or in the flesh. The first is this: you either operate in the realm of faith or in the realm of fear, either in God's mode of operation or Satan's mode of operation. To walk in the spirit, you must operate in faith. You may ask yourself, "Is it possible to walk in the spirit constantly?" The answer is, " Yes." It depends on you, it depends on your choices and for you to make the right choices, you must depend on the Holy Spirit, and the Word of God must be the measuring tool of all your decisions and choices. If God's anointing is on your life, you are fearless and bold, and you operate automatically in faith.

The second principle determining whether you walk in the spirit or in the flesh is that your spirit is either influenced by the Holy Spirit or by evil spirits. God does not divide things into secular and spiritual. Walking in the spirit realizes a total unity in your being: spirit, mind and body. Your life stops being fragmented and becomes whole.

Here are some examples from the Bible:
"Through the Spirit they urged Paul not to go on to Jerusalem." (Acts 21:4 NIV). Paul did not listen and went anyway to Jerusalem. He walked in the flesh and had to bear the consequences. Nevertheless God did not abandon him. On that occasion Paul missed God's perfect will for his life.

> In the temple courts he found men selling cattle, sheep and doves,
> and others sitting at tables exchanging money. So he made a whip
> out of cords, and drove all from the temple area, both sheep and
> cattle; he scattered the coins of the money changers and overturned
> their tables. To those who sold doves he said, "Get these out of here!
> How dare you turn my Father's house into a market!" (John 2:14–16
> NIV).

Here we see Jesus as a very angry man, yet He still walked in the spirit. By acting the way He did, He fulfilled the Scriptures. "...zeal for your house consumes me" (Psalm 69:9 NIV).

"Has this house, which bears my Name, become a den of robbers to you?" (Jeremiah 7:11 NIV).

Adam and Eve walked constantly in the spirit until the day they disobeyed God. "The man and his wife were both naked, and they felt no shame" (Genesis 2:25 NIV). They operated in perfect liberty, freedom and love.

"Then the eyes of both of them were opened, and they realized they were naked" (Genesis 3:7 NIV). This happened after the fall. Now they walked in the flesh, and by doing so, they operated in Satan's mode of fear instead of God's mode of faith.

He answered, "I heard you in the garden, and I was afraid because I was naked; so I hid" (Genesis 3:10 NIV). Fear entered the human heart for the first time. Let me give an example where most people think that they walk in the flesh. A born-again, Spirit-filled couple can have the liberty, freedom and peace Adam and Eve enjoyed before they disobeyed God, in their sexual relationship with each other. And, yes, they can walk in the spirit during that special time of their sexual-communion encounters.

Worshiping in Spirit and Truth

What does it mean to worship in spirit and truth? Worshiping in spirit means you must walk in the spirit as specified in the previous section. Those who worship in truth are the sons and daughters of God, who activate their obligations towards their God. It implies constant fellowship with God the Father, God the Son and God the Holy Spirit.

You must entertain a loving relationship with the Holy Spirit. "It is He who guides you into all truth" (John 16:13 NIV paraphrased). Without him you cannot understand the Word of God because it is spiritually discerned.

"The man without the Spirit does not accept the things that come from the Spirit of God, for they are foolishness to him, and he cannot understand them, because they are spiritually discerned" (1 Corinthians 2:14 NIV). There are certain things that must be avoided concerning the Word of God, the absolute truth.

You must entertain a loving relationship with the Son of God, Jesus Christ. Jesus is the way, the only way, to eternal life. He is the shepherd of his sheep.

> The man who enters by the gate is the shepherd of his sheep. The watchman opens the gate for him, and the sheep listen to his voice. He calls his own sheep by name and leads them out. When he has brought out all his own, he goes on ahead of them, and his sheep follow him because they know his voice. They will never follow a stranger; in fact, they will run away from him because they do not recognize a stranger's voice" (John 10:2–5 NIV).

A true believer will not be deceived by Satan's voice but will only listen to Jesus Christ the true shepherd.

The born-of -God believers must walk as Jesus walked.

> The man who says, "I know him," but does not do what he commands is a liar, and the truth is not in him. But if anyone obeys his word, God's love is truly made complete in him. This is how we know we are in him: Whoever claims to live in him must walk as Jesus did" (1 John 2:4–6 NIV).

"The Son is the radiance of God's glory and the exact representation of his being, sustaining all things by his powerful word" (Hebrews 1:3 NIV).

His powerful word enables us to take part in His divine nature. "Through these he has given us his very great and precious promises, so that through them you may participate in the divine nature" (2 Peter 1:4 NIV).

Through Jesus Christ, the sons and daughters of God Almighty will have power and authority to live a deception-free life.

You must entertain a loving relationship with the Father. What makes someone a father are his children. Every human being has two fathers: a natural, physical father and a spiritual father. For a born-of-God believer, that spiritual father is God the Father. "How much more should we submit to the Father of our spirits and live!" (Hebrews 12:9 NIV).

"I will be a Father to you, and you will be my sons and daughters, says the Lord Almighty" (2 Corinthians 6:18 NIV).

For not born-of-God believers, their spirit is dead and therefore the devil is their spiritual father. "You belong to your father, the devil, and you want to carry out your father's desire (John 8:44 NIV).

We must love, honor, respect and worship our heavenly Father. "Yet a time is coming and has now come when the true worshipers will worship the Father in spirit and truth, for they are the kind of worshipers the Father seeks" (John 4:23 NIV).

"Rather, worship the Lord your God; it is he who delivers you from the hand of all your enemies" (2 King 17:39 NIV).

Removing All Barriers

One must be aware not to raise up barriers between oneself and the Holy Spirit, Jesus and the Father. When barriers are in place, God feels distant to you. Unforgiveness is such a barrier, especially when you were wronged. It does not matter who wronged you. Love your enemies is a command of God not a voluntary option. A relative of one of the Green River killer's victims said on national television, "I forgive you, but you made it very hard for me to follow the command of my God."

Lack of unity among Christians, a family or a local Church is another barrier. Divine grace is bestowed on those who assemble in unity, who live in unity. It is called the sacrament of unity.

Lack of genuine love among people, which may stem from ethnic differences, skin color, education, physical appearances, etc. may be the greatest barrier one can erect, They should never divide us, but bring us closer together in love and harmony.

Disobedience to the Holy Spirit will prevent you from walking in the spirit and in the will, the perfect will, of God. You will be wasting your time and effort when you disobey.

There are many levels in Phase One, the Love Your God Phase. It is a progressive, maturing process. You cannot skip Phase One and go to Phase Two, the Love Others Phase. To be really successful in Phase Two depends entirely upon how successful you are in Phase One.

> Many will say to me that day, 'Lord, Lord, did we not prophesy in your name, and in your name drive out demons and perform many miracles? Then I will tell them plainly, 'I never knew you. Away from me you evildoers!'" (Matthew 7:22–23 NIV).

Those people operated in Phase Two but never took time to love their God. Phase One is to get to know Him by experiencing Him, by loving Him. Love your God Phase will never become obsolete or accomplished totally as long as a person lives, and that is eternal, because any born-of-God believer lives forever. In fact, this phase has a start but no end unless you end it.

The Love Others Phase

"Love one another. As I have loved you, so you must love one another. By this all men will know that you are my disciples, if you love one another" (John 13:34–35 NIV).

"Love your neighbor as yourself" (Mark 12:31 NIV).

Love for enemies: love does not repay evil for evil. "Love your enemies, do good to those who hate you, bless those who curse you, pray for those who mistreat you" (Luke 6:27–28 NIV).

The Love Others Phase requires good works on your part. The verse, "Man is justified by faith alone" (Romans 3:28 NIV paraphrased) has no value in this phase.

It has to be understood in context with other verses like, "Man is not justified by faith alone for faith without deeds, works is dead." (James 2:24–26 NIV paraphrased).

Also in the context of the verse, "You are predestined in Christ Jesus to do good works" (Ephesians 2:10 NIV paraphrased). What was Jesus doing on earth? He was doing good, and that is what every Christian is supposed to be doing: doing good. That requires action, deeds and works. This is the interpersonal spiritual intelligence or the interpersonal spiritual ability. It is the phase where a new dimension is added to your life. You are in Christ. It will not happen without you; it is your responsibility. You in Christ are unlimited because Jesus Christ is unlimited.

As a young boy I used to hang around the local blacksmith. Every day I was supposed to go to church before school, but during the winter months, I skipped church and went with some of my friends to the forge instead. For us boys, the forge was much more interesting than the daily mass. It always fascinated us to see a solid piece of iron turned into a useful tool. Four elements were needed to achieve that: wind, fire, oil and the hammer. The wind was needed to get the fire going, and the fire brought the iron to a red-hot glimmer. At that point, the iron piece was ready to be hammered into the desired shape. Lastly, it was dipped into the oil to harden it. I like to use this natural work and transpose it to the spiritual realm. The wind is a symbol of the Holy Spirit. He will put you through the fire, which will remove all the chaff from your life; it will refine and purify you. You are shaped by the Father through the Word of God (Jesus) into a useful instrument.

"The Word became flesh and made his dwelling among us" (John 1:14 NIV).

"'Is not my word like fire,' declares the Lord, 'and like a hammer that breaks a rock in pieces?'" (Jeremiah 23:29 NIV).

As the iron had to be dipped into oil, so you must be dipped into the oil, which means you must be anointed to be of any value. It can be very painful to be on the anvil, but you must not get off prematurely, not till the whole process is finalized. Only then will you be ready to be used by the Holy Spirit. You have become an invaluable instrument in the hands of the Holy Spirit to do what He wants you to do. You are a mature Christian with power.

Any life, be it the natural or the spiritual, is not static but dynamic, you do not regress but progress, you cannot be stagnant but must go forward. You must eat and drink daily to replenish your physical body. Your spirit is not any different. What you do not have, you cannot give. Daily, you must replenish your spirit, you must drink of the Holy Spirit."...and we were all given the one Spirit to drink" (1 Corinthians 12:13 NIV).

Rivers of Living Waters

You must drink daily of the Spirit; otherwise you run the risk of going dry, and you will no longer be able to give to others. You do not just drink for yourself but also for others. 1 Corinthians 12:13 is used in connection with the body of Christ. You cannot give to others what you yourself do not have.

"'Whoever believes in me, as the Scripture has said, streams of living water will flow from within him.' By this he meant the Spirit" (John 7:38–39 NIV).

It is very clear that unless you drink of the Spirit, the Spirit cannot flow out of you. Streams plural, not just one stream will flow out of you. What are those streams? They are streams of water: the Word of God, streams of fire, streams of oil: the anointing, and streams of light: Jesus flowing out of you. There is a sequence you must follow. You cannot jump and miss one. The streams stop flowing when you stop giving, when you stop loving others. The streams become stagnant and putrefaction sets in. The streams dry out when you stop drinking of the Spirit. Drinking of the Spirit keeps you in shape spiritually speaking and enables you to love other people. You become the hands, the feet, the mouth, the ears, the eyes and especially the heart of Jesus.

Do not try to dig your own well and drink of the world instead of the Spirit. "...They have forsaken me, the spring of living water, and have dug their own cisterns, broken cisterns that cannot hold water" (Jeremiah 2:13 NIV).

The Holy Spirit has no way of getting to the unsaved with His saving power except through the instrument of those of us who are already mature Christians: anointed ones. We become perfect vessels through which the Holy Spirit can work, the salvation plan of the human race. We are responsible for other people. If we do not yield our body, submit our mind and surrender our spirit to the Holy Spirit, He cannot act upon the unbeliever. We will be held responsible for the lost. We cannot simply bury our talent; we are our brothers' keeper.

Anointed to Serve

Fifty years ago, you hardly heard anything about the anointing, only occasionally in connection with the ordination of a priest or a minister. Nowadays, however, that has changed drastically. The anointing is for everybody who believes in Jesus Christ. Christ means the anointed one and Christians derive their name from it. A true Christian is anointed to serve. The anointing is for every Christian and not just for kings, priests and prophets.

What Is the Anointing?

The anointing is God's very power entrusted upon a person to enable that person to witness to all the world through the gifts of the Holy Spirit. Spiritual and natural gifts are those by which that person ministers to his or her fellow men and women. Once anointed with the Holy Spirit and with power, you become God's very own; you are set apart and commissioned for service. Oil is the symbol of the anointing. It flows from the top of your head to the bottom of your feet.

Let's look at Jesus, how He was anointed and for what purpose. We as Jesus' representatives are anointed in the same manner and for the same purpose.

> "The Spirit of the Lord is on me, because he has anointed me to preach good news to the poor. He has sent me to proclaim freedom for the prisoners and recovery of sight for the blind, to release the oppressed, to proclaim the year of the Lord's favor" (Luke 4:18–19 NIV).

"—how God anointed Jesus of Nazareth with the Holy Spirit and with power, and how he went around doing good and healing all who were under the power of the devil, because God was with him" (Acts 10:38 NIV).

Who Anoints You?

The anointing is the anointing of the Holy Spirit and it is performed by the Lord Jesus Christ. He has given you power, in His name. Unless you are anointed, nothing will happen.

To be anointed the following conditions must first be fulfilled.

- You must be trustworthy. When the Holy Spirit can trust you, you are a candidate.
- You must walk in the spirit and not in the flesh. You must operate in faith, God's mode of operation, and not in fear, Satan's mode of operation.
- You must yield your body, submit your mind and surrender your spirit to the Holy Spirit.
- Jesus must be formed in you by the Holy Spirit.
- You must walk in obedience to God, and, of course, you must want the anointing, and you must want to witness to the world.

Apart from people, God anoints things and places. These are always related to anointed people. The anointing may leave unless you constantly fulfill the conditions mentioned above. It is the price you have to pay. You should never harm an anointed person or mishandle an anointed object or an anointed place. Once you are anointed, you cannot go back. It would be the worst thing that could happen to a Christian. When the Holy Spirit left Saul, the anointing left him too, and he was tormented by an evil spirit. Destruction and death was the end result. "But the Lord forbid that I should lay a hand on the Lord's anointed" (1 Samuel 26:11 NIV).

> It is impossible for those who have once been enlightened, who have tasted the heavenly gift, who have shared in the Holy Spirit, who have tasted the goodness of the word of God and the powers of the coming age, if they fall away, to be brought back to repentance, because to their loss they are crucifying the Son of God all over again and subjecting him to public disgrace (Hebrews 6:4–6 NIV).

> "At that time the kingdom of heaven will be like ten virgins who took their lamps and went out to meet the bridegroom. Five of them were foolish and five were wise. The foolish ones took their lamps but did not take any oil with them. The wise, however, took oil in jars along with their lamps. The bridegroom was a long time in coming, and they all became drowsy and fell asleep.

> "At midnight the cry rang out: 'Here's the bridegroom! Come out to meet him!'

> "Then all the virgins woke up and trimmed their lamps. The foolish ones said to the wise, 'Give us some of your oil; our lamps are going out.'

"'No,' they replied, 'there may not be enough for both us and you. Instead, go to those who sell oil and buy some for yourselves.'

"But while they were on their way to buy the oil, the bridegroom arrived. The virgins who were ready went in with him to the wedding banquet. And the door was shut.

"Later the others also came, ' Sir! Sir!' they said. 'Open the door for us!'

"But he replied, 'I tell you the truth, I don't know you.'

"Therefore keep watch, because you do not know the day or the hour" (Matthew 25:1–13 NIV).

This parable reminds us that we cannot rely on others for the anointing. Every believer is responsible for his own anointing. You cannot rely on somebody else's anointing. At all times, you must be ready to serve others. The minute you keep the anointing for yourself, it ceases to flow. The stern rebuke of the bridegroom, "I don't know you," makes it very clear that when you are anointed, you cannot sit back while the world is dying and heading for eternal damnation.

"Many will say to me in that day, 'Lord, Lord, did we not prophesy in your name, and in your name drive out demons and perform many miracles?' Then I will tell them plainly, 'I never knew you. Away from me you evildoers!'" (Matthew 7:22–23 NIV).

Obviously those people were anointed at some time but lost it.

The Gifts of the Holy Spirit

A gift is freely given. You do not pay for it, you do not work for it and often you do not deserve it. There are spiritual and natural gifts; they do not compete with each other but complement each other. The gifts of the Holy Spirit find their field of operation in the six-fold ministry, namely: the ministry of helps, the ministry of the apostles, the ministry of the prophets, the ministry of the evangelists, the ministry of the pastors and the ministry of the teachers. These ministries are gifts by themselves. One could compare the six-fold ministry to an army with the Holy Spirit as the high command, the apostles, evangelists and prophets as the officers, the pastors and teachers as the sous-officers and the ministry of helps as the troops. As a believer you are part of the troops. A soldier does not take vacations, nor can he desert his post. If he does, he will be shot. Are you, the believer, still at your post, or did you take a permanent vacation? If you are still at your post, are you armed and equipped properly? If you do not put on your spiritual armor, you are naked, and if you do not operate in the gifts of the Spirit, you do not carry any weapons either. Pray that the enemy will laugh himself to death when seeing you.

> "It was he who gave some to be apostles, some to be prophets, some to be evangelists, and some to be pastors and teachers, to prepare God's people for works of service, [the ministry of helps] so that the body of Christ may be built up until we all reach unity in the faith and in the knowledge of the Son of God and become mature, attaining to the whole measure of the fullness of Christ" (Ephesians 4:11–13 NIV).

Every person is called by God to serve, nevertheless few are chosen. The calling is universal, but the choosing depends on you. You must fulfill certain conditions for God to choose you.

The ministry of helps is, number wise, the most important ministry. Actually, billions of people should be in this ministry worldwide. In comparison, it is equal to the ministry of the apostle, the prophet, the evangelist, the pastor and the teacher. The bulk of the work is accomplished by the ministry of helps. It is the workhorse, the backbone, so to speak. Without it, very little can be achieved by the others.

> "He who receives you receives me, and he who receives me receives the one who sent me. Anyone who receives a prophet because he is a prophet will receive a prophet's reward, and anyone who receives a righteous man because he is a righteous man will receive a righteous man's reward. And if anyone gives even a cup of cold water to one of these little ones because he is my disciple, I tell you the truth, he will certainly not lose his reward" (Matthew 10:40–42 NIV).

This makes it clear; in God's eyes if you work in the ministry of helps for an evangelist you will receive an evangelist's reward. The ministry of helps is active in your family, your work place, your community, your local church and all of the ministries of the apostle, the prophet, the evangelist, the pastor and teacher. Many will stay in the ministry of helps for life; few will be chosen by God to the other ministries as the Holy Spirit sees fit. While active in the ministry of helps, you are being pruned, hammered on the anvil, into a useful believer and worker. It is a time of heart circumcision, a time of character building. Out of the ministry of helps come the apostle, the prophet, the evangelist, the pastor and the teacher. The importance of the ministry of helps cannot be overemphasized. It is here where the training takes place. If you desire to become a pastor and are not active in the ministry of helps, you are fooling yourself. You may be a pastor but a dead one, a thimble Christian at best.

"So Elijah went from there and found Elisha son of Shaphat. He was plowing with twelve yoke of oxen, and he himself was driving the twelfth pair. Elijah went up to him and threw his cloak around him" (1 Kings 19:19 NIV).

> So he asked Jesse, "Are these all the sons you have?"
> "There is still the youngest," Jesse answered, "but he is tending the sheep."
> Samuel said, "Send for him; we will not sit down until he arrives."
> So he sent and had him brought in. He was ruddy, with a fine appearance and handsome features.
> Then the Lord said, "Rise and anoint him; he is the one" (1 Samuel 16:11–12 NIV).

"Now Jesus himself was about thirty years old when he began his ministry" (Luke 3:23 NIV). This clearly indicates Jesus was involved in the ministry of helps for at least eighteen years prior to his full-time ministry. Nowadays we call the ministry of helps ministry in the marketplace, the place where you have influence as a housewife, as a worker, as a politician, etc. Jesus was obedient to His earthly parents (Luke 2:51 NIV) and even more so to His heavenly Father. "Didn't you know I had to be in my Father's house?" (Luke 2:49 NIV). One can conclude with certainty that Jesus was active in the marketplace of His days, which prepared Him for His teaching ministry that culminated in his crucifixion and resurrection.

The gifts are given to witness to the people and to build the church, the bride of Christ.

> There are different kinds of gifts, but the same Spirit. There are different kinds of service, but the same Lord. There are different kinds of working, but the same God works all of them in all men. Now to each one the manifestation of the Spirit is given for the common good. To one there is given through the Spirit the message of wisdom, to another the message of knowledge by means of the same Spirit, to another faith by the same Spirit, to another gifts of

healing by that one Spirit, to another miraculous powers, to another prophecy, to another distinguishing between spirits, to another speaking in different kinds of tongues, and to still another the interpretation of tongues. All these are the work of one and the same Spirit, and he gives them to each one, just as he determines" (1 Corinthians 12:4–11 NIV).

The revelation gifts are wisdom, knowledge and discerning of spirits. The power gifts are faith, healing and miracles. The vocal gifts are tongues, interpretation of tongues and prophecy.

The gift of wisdom is an instruction to a person or persons for the present or for the future in relation to marriage, family, friends, job, ministry, finances, relationships, health, etc., to avoid disaster, to come out of a difficult situation or to make excellent and to build up. It can be for your body, mind or spirit.

The gift of knowledge is a message to a person or persons from the past or from the present. It can be something that the person does not know, like a disease or sickness, or something that the person knows, like having had an abortion in the past. The gift of knowledge is not to expose a person but to bring that person to a place where the Holy Spirit or Jesus can touch him or her.

The discerning of spirits is a gift enabling a person to distinguish between good and evil spirits. It is a badly needed gift today. Many so called Christians attack the work of the Holy Spirit, thinking it is from the devil. On the other hand, they believe doctrines taught by demons. This gift also enables you to know what spirit you are dealing with, like a lying spirit, a deceiving spirit, etc.

The gift of faith is different from the measure of faith that every human being received. Your measure of faith enables you to operate in faith, in God's mode of operation, while the gift of faith is a power set into motion for a person who is unable to activate his own measure of faith. Remember nothing happens in the spiritual realm unless faith is present; it is the way God operates.

The gift of healing, through it a person is healed (from sickness and disease) in his body, mind or spirit.

The gift of miracles supersedes the natural laws. For instance, you have only one leg and a new leg grows, you have no eyes and a pair of eyes is created in your eye sockets, you are in a fierce fire but you come out not a hair singed or a person may be dead but that person can be brought back to life. There is no limit to the gift of miracles.

The gift of tongues is plural because there are different modalities of tongues. You speak in tongues, your spiritual language, to God, or while speaking in tongues, a person or persons hear you speak in their native language. Other times you speak in your native language and a person or persons hear you in their native language.

Speaking in Tongues

Every born of God believer has a spiritual language. Unfortunately most of them are mute because they do not know that they have a spiritual language. Their language is inactive and dormant. The spiritual language is called speaking in tongues. "All of them were filled with the Holy Spirit and began to speak in other tongues as the Spirit enabled them" (Acts 2:4 NIV). For anyone who speaks in a tongue does not speak to men but to God. Indeed, no one understands him; he utters mysteries with his spirit and his mind (physical mind) is unfruitful. No two believers utter the same words; it is as personal as your fingerprints.

To understand the spiritual language, one must comprehend the basic principle of how God's word works. The written word of God, contained in the Bible and lying on the shelf, accomplishes nothing. But when that word is spoken by a believer (whose heart operates in faith and who acts in the authority of Jesus) that word is endued with power, activated and accomplishes what it is supposed to accomplish. Life and death are in the power of the tongue.

The spiritual language is a gift of the Holy Spirit. It is He who guides you, enables you and puts power into your speaking. The spiritual language must be spoken by your physical body to cause a spiritual or natural event to occur, to change its course or to prevent it from happening in the spiritual or natural realm. Why do we have to speak it? Because we, as humans, are in authority here on earth.

Speaking in tongues is like sending out a carrier wave, and the Holy Spirit is superimposing the characteristics of signals onto that carrier wave and directing it to where it is supposed to go, and it will accomplish its task. The good thing about this is we will not get in God's way and Satan and his demons cannot listen in. Here are but a few examples of what speaking in tongues does, but keep in mind God is not limited unless we limit Him.

When you speak in tongues you are speaking divine mysteries "...he utters mysteries with his spirit" (1 Corinthians 14:2 NIV). What are those mysteries?

"...we speak of God's secret wisdom, a wisdom that has been hidden and that God destined for our glory before time began" (1 Corinthians 2:7 NIV). In the Bible, the wisdom of God often refers to the plan of God on the earth. It keeps God's plans concealed from the enemy, Satan. Keeping the devil in the dark about what God is doing is very important. 1 Corinthians 2:8 illustrates this very well. "None of the rulers of this age understood it, for if they had, they would not have crucified the Lord of Glory" (NIV).

As you pray in tongues, secrets will be revealed to you, Spirit to spirit. You are praying God's plan for your life, for the life of others, for the implementation of God's Kingdom here on the earth and for the destruction of Satan's work.

> We have not received the spirit of the world but the Spirit who is from God, that we may understand what God has freely given us. This is what we speak [in tongues], not in words taught us by human wisdom but in words taught by the Spirit, expressing spiritual truths in spiritual words (1 Corinthians 2:12–13 NIV).

When you don't know what or how you should pray, tongues are the answer. If you don't have sufficient knowledge or information in order to pray intelligently, you can pray in the Spirit, confident that He will pray through you. "In the same way, the Spirit helps us in our weakness [inability]. We do not know what we ought to pray for, but the Spirit himself intercedes for us with groans that words cannot express" (Romans 8:26 NIV).

Refreshing, edifying or re-strengthening is yet another facet of speaking in tongues.

> Very well then, with foreign lips and strange tongues God will speak to his people, to whom he said, "This is the resting place, let the weary rest"; and, "This is the place of repose"—but they would not listen (Isaiah 28:11–12 NIV).

"He who speaks in a tongue edifies himself" (1 Corinthians 14:4 NIV).

By now you may wonder, "How do I get started?" Speaking or praying in tongues is an act of your will. God does not and will not override your will. You are a free person and you must take the initiative if you are going to speak in tongues. Too many people think the Holy Spirit will suddenly pounce on them and take control of their vocal cords. This is not how God operates. You don't have to try all kinds of things either. Here is how you go about it. Ask for the gift of tongues and then take the initiative.

Start praying, but not in words that you understand. Simply exercise your will to make an utterance and allow the Holy Spirit to shape it. The Holy Spirit will develop your prayer language as you yield your body to Him, as you submit your mind to Him and as you surrender your spirit to Him. At the back of your mind you may think "This is just me, I am making this up." Of course it is you. It is your spirit being spoken to and through by the Holy Spirit. The proof of the Holy Spirit's involvement comes as you are edified, built up and refreshed. You will know then that it's not just you.

The interpretation of tongues occurs when you speak in your spiritual language and another person translates your spiritual language into a human language such as French, English, etc.

The gift of prophecy is a message to a person or persons for the future and is usually conditional. God always reveals the future to his people.

If you are a full-time minister, all the gifts should be operational in your life. The best gift is the one needed in a particular situation at a specific time. Function determines structure. If you do not use the gifts they become non-operational.

"For God's gifts and his call are irrevocable" (Romans 11:29 NIV). God does not take his gifts back or withdraw the calling on your life, but through your fault and wrong choices, the gifts may become non-operational and it is up to you to follow God's calling.

The gifts are for the common good, not for your prestige or for your financial gain. Any believer should eagerly desire the gifts of the Holy Spirit and put himself in a position to receive those gifts. Nevertheless, there are some conditions to be fulfilled to be a candidate. You must be able to yield your body, submit your mind and surrender your spirit to the Holy Spirit. You must put your natural gifts to good use in the service of others. If those natural gifts are buried, how can you expect the Holy Spirit to give you spiritual gifts when you are a bad steward of your natural gifts and talents?

The Holy Spirit is the great orchestra for God's saving plan of mankind. He gives the gifts to different people to do specific tasks. It is not for us to pick out some field of service and then ask the Holy Spirit to qualify us for that service. It is not for us to select some gifts and ask the Holy Spirit to impart to us these self-chosen gifts except for the gift of tongues. The gift of tongues is different from all other gifts in that it is for every believer who has received the Holy Spirit. But you still have to ask for it. It is up to us to simply put ourselves at the disposal of the Holy Spirit to send us where He wills, to select for us what kind of service He wills and to impart to us what gift(s) He wills.

"God also testified to it by signs, bold wonders and various miracles, and gifts of the Holy Spirit distributed according to his will" (Hebrews 2:4 NIV).

Total Communion

This paragraph is the most important one for your life. It is also the most difficult one to write about. Total communion, between husband and wife in marriage, is strictly between the two. A third person would spoil everything. The intimacy they share among themselves is not meant to be divulged by any means.

No two persons are alike. No two relationships between a person and the Holy Spirit are alike either.

"May the grace of the Lord Jesus Christ, and the love of God, and the fellowship of the Holy Spirit be with you all" (2 Corinthians 13:14 NIV). The Bible only mentions 'the fellowship of the Holy Spirit' twice. This verse varies from Bible version to Bible version in particular the word 'fellowship'. The German version says, *die Hilfe* (the help), the Spanish version says, *la presencia constante* (the constant presence) and the French version says, *la communion* (the communion). It stems from the difficulty to translate the original into a Western language that does not have a single word rendering the same meaning.

The Amplified version seems to accommodate all the meanings. "The grace (favor and spiritual blessing) of the Lord Jesus Christ and the love of God and the presence and fellowship (the communion and sharing together and participation) in the Holy Spirit be with you all" (2 Corinthians 13:14 AMB). The word communion conveys best the original meaning. What is communion? Communion means the following:

- *Yielding your body, submitting your mind and surrendering your spirit to the Holy Spirit.* There is neither rebellion nor resistance in you.

- *Respect* for each other, for what He is, for what you are, the sum total of you. Nothing should destroy that respect. The Holy Spirit respects you so much that He will never barge in. He is a gentleman. He never coerces you. You must welcome Him every day.

- *Fellowship, companionship, friendship.* He is your best friend. Any time you can ask Him for help, He is always there when you need Him. There will be no hidden secrets between you. You confide the most secret things to Him and He will reveal the deep things of God to you. "The Spirit searches all things, even the deep things of God" (1 Corinthians 2:10 NIV).

- *Participation and sharing* involves taking part in the life of the other person and having in common work, interests and whatever you hold dear.

- *Love,* at its best, is total intimacy, consideration, tact, thoughtfulness, and complete unselfishness. Thoughts and feelings exchange, His friends are your friends, His enemies are your enemies.

Communion does not happen at a distance, both persons have to be close. Communion with the Holy Spirit changes you more than anything else, and it motivates you for holiness. Holiness is not just absence of sin but truthfulness and perfection in every respect. Communion raises you to a higher status; you walk constantly in the spirit. The world no longer attracts you; your desires change. You no longer worry what people may think of you. You become unimportant to yourself and your opinion no longer is an idol to you. You want to please Him, to be with Him and to do what He wants you to do.

Both phases should be part of every Christian's life. For a true, mature Christian, operating in love must become a way of life. Some Christians may primarily operate in Phase One, others in Phase Two, but all should operate to some extent in both phases.

> As Jesus and his disciples were on their way, he came to a village where a woman named Martha opened her home to him. She had a sister called Mary, who sat at the Lord's feet listening to what he said. But Martha was distracted by all the preparations that had

to be made. She came to him and asked, "Lord, don't you care that my sister has left me to do the work by myself?' Tell her to help me!"

"Martha, Martha," the Lord answered, "you are worried and upset about many things, but only one thing is needed. Mary has chosen what is better, and it will not taken away from her" (Luke 10:38–41 NIV).

Martha and Mary illustrate both phases perfectly.

God calls dedicated men and women to implement His redemptive work among people. Some are like Martha, others like Mary. The Sisters of Mother Teresa of Calcutta operate in both Phases. The Sisterhood of Mary, a Protestant women's order, operates primarily in Phase One. There are so-called active orders of men and women and contemplative orders of men and women. Contemplative orders encourage their members to seek union and communion with God through love but by seclusion and freedom from the worldly spirit, thus the objective worship of God is perfected. In purpose, it is a continuous life of prayer to God that His kingdom may flourish and dying to oneself in consolation to Jesus Christ for reparation of the many people who not only neglect to worship God but through their lifestyle greatly sadden Him. They wipe the tears of Jesus in solitude and silence.

On the other hand, there is the active apostolate, which must rely on the contemplative apostolate to be of any success. Romans 12:4 tells us that not all members have the same function. Most missionary orders are active orders. They build churches, schools, hospitals, etc. to implement a social structure in which they can impact the local population and win them for Jesus Christ.

There is a Catholic order I am very familiar with. It is called, The Fathers of the Sacred Heart of Jesus. It is partly a contemplative and partly an active apostolate including missionary work. It stresses the worship of Jesus for His love represented by His heart. The worship is centered on reparation to Christ for men's ingratitude manifested particularly by indifference to the Holy Eucharist. The worship is not directed to the heart alone but to the person of Jesus Christ.

6. Ways and Means of God's Action

Through the death on the cross and resurrection of Jesus Christ, men's redemption from eternal damnation was brought about. The work is finished. It belongs to all mankind. It is there for the taking. Mankind is not saved automatically, but each individual must ask for it. God never forces anybody to receive and accept Him. Because of peoples' free will, they can either accept or reject Him. That decision determines where they will spend eternity—either in heaven with God and His angels or in hell with Satan and his demons—either in God's kingdom or in Satan's kingdom.

Mankind is so privileged to have the option to become a son or a daughter of God and to be empowered to live a victorious life and to be a source of life for others. Often we become insensitive to the eternal spiritual reality we are part of and neglect to achieve our full potential as a Christian. Christian life was never meant to be difficult; in fact, it ought to be easy and down to earth, and it can be like that as long as we remember some simple principles to understand how God dispenses His grace (divine influence) to people. Here are some basic principles every Christian ought to know and understand.

Authority

Who is in authority on the earth? God? No, it is mankind. Adam and Eve were given total authority and dominion on the earth from God. Through their fall, Satan appropriated that dominion for himself.

> The devil led him up to a high place and showed him in an instant all the kingdoms of the world. And he said to him, "I will give you all their authority and splendor, for it has been given to me, and I can give it to anyone I want to. So if you worship me, it will all be yours" (Luke 4:5–7 NIV).

> Jesus the Son of Man took that authority back from Satan through His death and resurrection and placed it back into the hands of mankind. "Then Jesus came to them and said, 'All authority in heaven and on earth has been given to me" (Matthew 28:18 NIV).

Jesus delegated that authority to you and me. Therefore, before God can interfere in men's affairs, He needs permission to do so. He needs the legal right from men to do so. That's the reason we must ask. Praying to God gives Him that legal right to intervene in our lives. The Scriptures are full of examples.

> Jesus stopped and said, "Call him."
>
> So they called to the blind man, "Cheer up! On your feet! He is calling you." Throwing his cloak aside, he jumped to his feet and came to Jesus.
>
> "What do you want me to do for you?" Jesus asked him.
>
> The blind man said, "Rabbi, I want to see."
>
> "Go," said Jesus, "your faith has healed you." Immediately he received his sight and followed Jesus along the road (Mark 10:49–52 NIV).

It was obvious that the man was blind, but Jesus had to ask him what he wanted Him to do for him. In other words, He asked for permission to impart God's grace to his life, the healing power to restore his sight. Many people never give Jesus the permission to heal them, to set them free, to deliver them, or to intervene in their lives, so they can live a victorious life. Who has power? How do power and authority come to us?

Power

Authority and power belong to the sons and daughters of God Almighty. "For the kingdom of God is not a matter of talk but of power" (1 Corinthians 4:20 NIV). For children of God, it is only natural to share in His power that will enable them to live a victorious life and to help others to do the same.

But a person must know that divine power is available to him or her. "Jesus replied, 'You are in error because you do not know the scriptures or the power of God'" (Matthew 22:29 NIV).

From the Father

God is omnipotent, all-powerful. "For since the creation of the world God's invisible qualities—his eternal power and divine nature– have been clearly seen, being understood from what has been made, so that men are without excuse" (Romans 1:20 NIV).

"...being fully persuaded that God had power to do what he had promised" (Romans 4:21 NIV). God the Father is the source of all power and authority. He has all power and authority in heaven and on earth.

Adam and Eve shared in that power and authority but lost it to Satan when they fell in the Garden of Eden. Man was in big trouble. He could not save himself, but God came to man's rescue, as He had promised Adam. God cannot, as such, redeem mankind. There has to be a perfect man who can take Adam's place.

Through Jesus Christ

So around the year A.D.1, God the Father sent His Son Jesus to earth. God became a man like you and me. He was stripped of all godly attributes while being here on earth. Since He was not an offspring of Adam, He was spiritually alive and became the perfect ransom for all mankind. When Satan tempted Jesus, he offered Him some of the power and authority.

> The devil led him up to a high place and showed him in an instant all the kingdoms of the world. And he said to him, "I will give you all their authority and splendor, for it has been given to me, and I can give it to anyone I want to. So if you worship me, it will all be yours."
>
> Jesus answered, "It is written: 'Worship the Lord your God and serve him only'" (Luke 4:5–8 NIV).

The devil could talk like that, because Adam had lost all authority to Satan in the Garden of Eden more than four thousand years ago.

This is what Jesus said after the resurrection, "All authority in heaven and on earth has been given to me" (Matthew 28:18 NIV).

"Go into all the world and preach the good news to all creation" (Mark 16:15 NIV). God's power and authority for mankind comes through Jesus Christ.

"…but to those whom God has called, both Jews and Greeks, Christ the power of God and the wisdom of God" (1 Corinthians 1:24 NIV).

"…and you have been given fullness in Christ, who is the head over every power and authority" (Colossians 2:10 NIV).

"At that time the sign of the Son of Man will appear in the sky, and all the nations of the earth will mourn. They will see the Son of Man coming on the clouds of the sky, with power and great glory" (Matthew 24:30 NIV).

The divine power and authority comes through three channels: the shed blood on Calvary, God's Word and the name of Jesus Christ.

Through the blood of Jesus, His death and resurrection.

"For the message of the cross is foolishness to those who are perishing, but to us who are being saved it is the power of God" (1 Corinthians 1:18 NIV). As believers, we can, at any given time, appropriate Jesus' blood for our benefit. It never loses its power. The blood will wash and cleanse us, justify and sanctify us, free us from sin, gives us peace and protection and bring us close to Jesus. The devil cannot stand it, he has to retreat. You speak it and believe it, and nothing that may harm you will come near your dwelling place.

Through the Word

Jesus Himself defeated Satan by using the Word of God ("It is written,") as narrated in Luke 4:1–13 (NIV).

"...because our gospel came to you not simply with words, but also with power, with the Holy Spirit and with deep conviction" (1 Thessalonians 1:5 NIV).

"The words I have spoken to you are spirit and they are life" (John 6:63 NIV).

"I am not ashamed of the gospel, because it is the power of God for the salvation of everyone who believes: first for the Jew, then for the Gentile (Romans 1:16 NIV).

Jesus declared things that were not as though they were. "He chose the lowly things of this world and the despised things—and the things that are not—to nullify the things that are, so that no one may boast before him" (1 Corinthians 1:28–29 NIV).

"He is our father in the sight of God, in whom he believed—the God who gives life to the dead and calls things which are not as though they were" (Romans 4:17 NIV). Things already existing in the spiritual realms are then manifested in the material world. As sons and daughters of God, we share in that creative power.

Through the name of Jesus

As a believer we operate constantly in the authority and power of God. How do we do it? We use the name of Jesus. We say, In the name of Jesus or in Jesus' name, and every devil or demon has to bow and obey us. When the king's seal is applied to a decree, it becomes law, and it does not matter who puts the seal on. It is a seal of authority when we use the name of Jesus. "I will remain in the world no longer, but they are still in the world, and I am coming to you. Holy Father, protect them by the power of your name—the name you gave me—so that they may be one as we are one" (John 17:11 NIV).

By the Holy Spirit

The power is not given to anyone randomly but with a purpose and a goal. It will never be dispensed for misuse. Without the Holy Spirit, no power will be manifested. "But you will receive power when the Holy Spirit comes on you; and you will be my witnesses in Jerusalem, and in all Judea and Samaria, and to the ends of the earth" (Acts 1:8 NIV).

"I am going to send you what my Father has promised; but stay in the city until you have been clothed with power from on high" (Luke 24:49 NIV).

That power is also called the anointing. It is the Holy Spirit in action through a believer. "Not by might nor by power, but by my Spirit, says the Lord Almighty" (Zechariah 4:6 NIV).

The power, the anointing and the authority of God are given for what purpose?

For every need in life
The power, the anointing and the authority of God are given for every need. "His divine power has given us everything we need for life and godliness through our knowledge of him who called us by his own glory and goodness" (2 Peter 1:3 NIV).

"I pray that out of his glorious riches he may strengthen you with power through his Spirit in your inner being" (Ephesians 3:16 NIV).

At work within us
God's power is at work within us. "Now to him who is able to do immeasurably more than all we ask or imagine, according to his power that is at work within us" (Ephesians 3:20 NIV).

Our faith rests on God's power

God's power is the key for our faith. "...so that your faith might not rest on men's wisdom, but on God's power" (1 Corinthians 2:5 NIV).

"...having been buried with him in baptism and raised with him through your faith in the power of God, who raised him from the dead" (Colossians 2:12 NIV).

"With this in mind, we constantly pray for you, that our God may count you worthy of his calling, and that by his power he may fulfill every good purpose of yours and every act prompted by your faith" (2 Thessalonians 1:11 NIV).

Power to get wealth

"It is he that giveth thee power to get wealth, that he may establish his covenant which he swore unto thy fathers, as it is this day" (Deuteronomy 8:18, King James, as cited in Strong, 1989).

Power to heal sickness and disease

God's power is given to us to heal and cure sickness and disease. "One day as he was teaching, Pharisees and teachers of the law, who had come from every village of Galilee and from Judea and Jerusalem, were sitting there. And the power of the Lord was present for him to heal the sick" (Luke 5:17 NIV).

"...and the people all tried to touch him, because power was coming from him and healing them all" (Luke 6:19 NIV).

Power to destroy all the power of the enemy

The believer is endowed with power to destroy the works of the enemy, to bring down strongholds, to cast out demons and to give orders to evil spirits who must obey those orders. "I have given you authority to trample on snakes and scorpions and to overcome all the power of the enemy; nothing will harm you" (Luke 10:19 NIV).

"The weapons we fight with are not the weapons of the world. On the contrary, they have divine power to demolish strongholds" (2 Corinthians 10:4 NIV).

"When Jesus had called the Twelve together, he gave them power and authority to drive out all demons and to cure diseases" (Luke 9:1 NIV). "All the people were amazed and said to each other, "What is this teaching? With authority and power he gives orders to evil spirits and they come out!" (Luke 4:36 NIV).

The inborn desire in humans to access the supernatural is used by Satan to substitute idolatry, witchcraft and Satanism for the real thing. They represent a counterfeit of the real power, God's power. They have a purpose to lure people away from the true God, thus preventing them from having life, sonship and power. Witchcraft and Satanism work evil. Anyone or anything a person puts ahead of the true God is idolatry. It will open a door for Satan and his demons to oppress and/or to possess those persons. Their final outcome is total destruction and death.

God does not bypass the established authority of apostles, prophets, evangelists, pastors, teachers, priests and ministers. Scriptures are full of examples to show how Jesus always submitted to that authority.

> Then Jesus came from Galilee to the Jordan to be baptized by John. But John tried to deter him, saying, 'I need to be baptized by you, and do you come to me?'
>
> Jesus replied, 'Let it be so now; it is proper for us to do this to fulfill all righteousness.' Then John consented (Matthew 3:13–15 NIV).

It is a divine order instituted and approved by God Almighty, and we humans do well to submit to that order. God's grace, spiritual and natural, always comes through matter, an earthen vessel. Jesus Himself had to become matter to accomplish mankind's redemption. That principle is still in effect today. The work of Jesus is accomplished, but the redemption has to be delivered to the respective persons now. The delivery of God's specific grace is also achieved through matter, an earthen vessel, a person. Even though, at times, that matter is unworthy, God's grace is still delivered and effective. Read Matthew 7:22–23.

God's grace, divine influence to nourish, to strengthen, to revive, to refresh, to give life, to set free, to deliver, and to heal spirit, mind and body is delivered by a person (matter), and the way that person delivers it is also accomplished by way of matter. Some people, including Martin Luther, think our physical nature is so corrupt and sinful nothing good comes out from it. Yet, it is the temple of the Holy Spirit, and God uses that physical nature (matter) always to bestow His grace upon His people.

God delights in using the foolish things of this world to confound the wise, and calls the things that are not as though they are. Close-minded religious people get offended and receive no grace because they reject God's ways.

> Having said this, he spit on the ground, made some mud with the saliva, and put it on the man's eyes. "Go," he told him, "wash in the Pool of Siloam'" (this word means Sent). So the man went and washed, and came home seeing" (John 9:6–7 NIV).

Here Jesus used spittle and mud to impart sight to a blind man's eyes. Matter can be basically anything; most common are water, oil, bread, wine, cloth, Jesus' blood and even shadow. The list is endless. The way matter is used is called form, which includes an action: laying on of hands, pointing, waving, blowing etc. coupled with spoken words. Spoken words by a man of God or a born-of-God believer are the most powerful matter one can use.

The Word of God

The greatest evil in the past was deception, and it still is today. To avoid being deceived one must rely on the Word of God—the Bible. Science is the art of discovering the truth—both in the material world and the spiritual world. The truth can only be found if one uses the Word of God as a guide and measuring stick.

Science can be defined as a body of data arrived at and validated by observation and repeated experimentation. Science and the Bible are not in opposition to one another. When the Word of God is rightly understood and science honestly pursued, they will corroborate one another and harmonize to establish truth. It is only when science gets off track or when religious tradition perverts the Bible that there seems to be a conflict.

The Italian astronomer, Galileo Galilei, is a concrete historical example of how religious tradition came into conflict with science. Galileo not only endorsed the Copernican theory that the Earth revolves around the Sun—not the Sun around the Earth, but even provided practical proof to support it. The church authority of the time (1616) declared the theory of Copernicus to be false and heretical, thus Galileo became a victim. He was charged with the Copernican heresy in 1633 and was forced under threat of torture to recant and spent the rest of his life under house arrest. His book, *Dialogue Concerning Two World Systems*, (1632) was placed on the Index of Forbidden Books.

The Bible clearly states that the earth is round and revolves around the sun. "He sits enthroned above the circle of the earth" (Isaiah 40:22 NIV). All that the church authority had to do was to read the Bible; even a child could have done it. They did not grasp the material truth, much less any spiritual truth. Jesus Christ taught His disciples for more than three years, yet they did not understand the spiritual truth. Only when the Holy Spirit came into their lives did they finally catch up. The understanding of the Bible is spiritually discerned. The Holy Spirit must reveal it to you.

Pope, John Paul II, apologized publicly to the world and in particular to the scientific community for all the wrong done to Galileo.

Satan is always on the lookout to defile, to distort and/or to substitute a lie for what God says in His Word. The Bible, the Will and Testament of God, the Book, the Scriptures, the Word of God or the Written Word of God all refer to the same thing. It is significant that a book is called the Word. It is the term I personally like the best.

"Man does not live on bread alone, but on every word that comes from the mouth of God" (Matthew 4:4 NIV). Our physical body needs food to nourish it and so does our spirit.
The Word is the food for our spirit. "The words I have spoken to you are spirit and they are life" (John 6:63 NIV).

The Word of God is not a set of stories, a history book or a compilation of guidelines for healthy living, even though it can be used that way, but a dynamic, powerful, living, perfect, eternal tool. Heaven and earth will pass away, but not God's word. It sustains all things, reveals God to us, works in those who believe, heals, preserves, strengthens, does good, cleanses, purifies, gives life, saves and comes with power. "...because our gospel came to you not simply with words, but also with power, with the Holy Spirit and with deep conviction" (1 Thessalonians 1:5 NIV).

The word of God is like a fire in your heart, it is a light to your path and a lamp to your feet. Here is what God says about His word,

> As the rain and the snow come down from heaven, and do not return to it without watering the earth and making it bud and flourish, so that it yields seed for the sower and bread for the eater, so is my word that goes out from my mouth: It will not return to me

empty, but will accomplish what I desire and achieve the purpose
for which I send it (Isaiah 55:10 NIV).

If a believer uses God's word, speaks it and believes it, it does the same thing as if God Himself spoke it.

"He has made us competent as ministers of a new covenant—not of the letter but of the Spirit; for the letters kills, but the Spirit gives life" (2 Corinthians 3:6 NIV). For the Word of God to be effective in your life you must have a loving relationship with the Holy Spirit; otherwise you run the risks of heresies and traditions.

Without Him, you cannot understand the Word of God, because it is spiritually discerned. "The man without the Spirit does not accept the things that come from the Spirit of God, for they are foolishness to him, and he cannot understand them, because they are spiritually discerned" (1 Corinthians 2:14 NIV).

The Word of God is the sword of the Spirit. It is not like a sword, but it is a real spiritual sword, much more effective than a material sword. At the time when the Word of God was written, the soldiers used a sword as their main personal, offensive and defensive weapon in fighting the enemy.

"Take the helmet of salvation and the sword of the Spirit, which is the word of God" (Ephesians 6:17 NIV).

Jesus used the sword of the Spirit remarkably while the devil tempted him in the desert (Matthew 4:1–11 NIV). At each attack of the devil he would say, "It is written..."quoting specific Bible verses appropriate for the situation. Each time he defeated and defused the devil's schemes. Nothing can withstand the Word of God. Jesus was successful, and so will you be, because the determining factor for success is the Holy Spirit. It is his sword Jesus used; it is His sword you are using.

When Martin Luther came on the scene he advocated the reading and study of the Bible. The Catholics, on the other hand, did the opposite. They refrained from reading and studying the Bible, because of Luther (1483–1546). They wanted nothing to do with him or his Protestant beliefs. Since the Catholics were at that time the major Christian church, it plunged the then known world into dark ages. This is a prime example of what happens when the Word of God is taken out of people's lives or from a nation.

The Book of the Bible

The Bible was written across a period of many centuries in the languages of Hebrew and Aramaic for the Old Testament and Greek for the New Testament. From this original text, ancient versions were reproduced by hand into Greek, Syiac and Latin.

The Septuagint

The Septuagint took its name from the Latin word for seventy, because there were seventy scholars involved in the translation. It is the oldest translation in the world. The Old Testament was translated from Hebrew into Greek for the Greek-speaking Jews living in Alexandria in Egypt. The Septuagint became the authorized version of the early Gentile church. To this day it is the official version of the Old Testament used in the Greek Orthodox Church.

The Syriac

The Syriac version is written in the Eastern Aramaic language, spoken by the people who lived in northern Mesopotamia.

The Coptic

The Christian community in Egypt saw fit to have the Bible translated into Coptic, a highly developed form of the native language of the ancient Egyptians.

The Gothic

Bishop Ulfilos brought the Good News to the Goths and translated the Bible for the new converts into Gothic. It was the first translation of the Bible into a language of the Germanic family, which also includes English, German, Dutch and Scandinavian.

The Latin

During the second century, when Latin replaced Greek as the dominant language of the Roman Empire, a Latin Bible was produced. The first Old Testament sections of that Bible were considered unreliable because it was a translation from a translation, the Septuagint.

The need for a better translation was obvious. Damasus, bishop of Rome (366–384), entrusted the task to his secretary Jerome. Jerome undertook the task unwillingly but produced a very good translation, which he completed in 405. It is know as the Latin Vulgate. It was through this Bible that the gospel arrived in Western Europe.

The division of the Bible into chapters is credited to Cardinal Stephen Langton, archbishop of Canterbury (1206). In 1546, the Council of Trent decreed that only this same ancient Vulgate edition be held as authoritative in public lectures, disputations, sermons and expository discourses. Until the twentieth century, no translations of the Bible except those based on the Vulgate were recognized as authoritative by the Catholic Church.

Pope Sixtus the Fifth (1585–1590) considered himself something of a scholar, and undertook a good deal of editorial work on the new edition of the Latin Bible for which the Council of Trent had called. The edition proofed so faulty that it was withdrawn a few days after the Pope's death.

The Geneva Bible
Many Englishmen were exiled and lived in Geneva during the early years of the reign of the Catholic Queen Mary (1535). A group of them produced a Bible called the Geneva Bible. It was the first Bible with numbered verses and the first English Bible to be entirely translated from the original biblical languages. It was the most widely read Bible until the King James Bible replaced it in 1611.

The King James
The King James Version was published in 1611, but was preceded by five other English versions: two Wycliffe versions, and the Tyndale, Coverdale and Matthew versions. With the invention of the printing press, the famous Gutenberg edition of the Latin Bible was the first major work to be printed. Martin Luther made the Bible available in German for the common people. He translated the New Testament into German in 1522 and the Old Testament into German in 1523. What Luther did for the German people, Tyndale did for the English people. Tyndale's Bibles were printed, not hand transcribed, and they were translated from their original languages and not from Latin. They were sold in England even though the church officially banned them. In May of 1535, Tyndale was arrested and imprisoned for seventeen months. He was then sentenced to death as a heretic; strangled and burned at the stake at Vilvorde, near Brussels on October 6, 1536. That was not an isolated incident. As early as the Christian persecutions, many were martyred and the Scriptures were burned.

The "Great Bible"
The "Great Bible" was authorized by King Henry VIII (1539). It was essentially a copy of Tyndale's translation revised by Coverdale. It was widely bought and read. The sudden access to Scriptures created such an excitement that King Henry issued new regulations limiting the reading of the Bible to wealthy merchants and the aristocrats.

With the rise of the reformation, all the books of the Reformers, including the Protestant Bibles, were placed in the Index of Prohibited Books (1545) by Pope Paul III. For a long time, merely to possess one of these banned books in Spain was punishable by death. The Index was kept up to date until 1959 but was finally abolished after four centuries by Pope Paul VI.

Books of the Bible
The Bible is divided into two chief parts: the 46 books of the Old Testament and the 27 books of the New Testament. The Old Testament was written over a period of about a thousand years and the New Testament over a period of one hundred years. The meaning of the word testament from both the Hebrew and the Greek languages is treaty or covenant. Covenant best captures the meaning of testament—Old Covenant and New Covenant.

Catholic and Protestant Bibles differ in that the Catholic Bibles contain the following fifteen extra books that the Protestant Bibles do not have:
 1. First Esdras
 2. Second Esdras
 3. Tobit
 4. Judith
 5. The Additions to Esther
 6. The Wisdom of Solomon
 7. Ecclesiasticus, or the Wisdom of Jesus, the Son of Sirach
 8. Baruch
 9. The Letter of Jeremiah
 10. The Prayer of Azariah and the Song of the Three Young Men
 11. Susanna
 12. Bel and the Dragon
 13. The Prayer of Manasseh
 14. First Maccabees
 15. Second Maccabees

The New Jerusalem Bible
The New Jerusalem Bible (1990) contains those extra fifteen books. The Jerusalem Bible (1966) is a scholarly production with a high degree of literacy skill. It is nonsectarian and is used by many denominations. The Catholics hold that these books are canonical and inspired by the Holy Spirit. The Catholics call books that are not canonical or inspired Apocrypha, and they are numerous. The Protestants call the same books Pseudopigrapha. Further the Protestants call the fifteen books contained in the Catholic Bibles Apocrypha.

Nowadays there are numerous new Bible versions, and the Bible is practically translated in every language and tongue.

The Sacraments

A sacrament is an outward sign established by Jesus Christ to confer inward grace by the power of the Holy Spirit. Sacraments are combinations of sacramentals in action. Sacramentals are types of matter used by men of God. They are the building blocks of sacraments. Sacraments are composed of essential elements. The first element is a sensible sign (sensed by the senses) instituted by God. The second is matter and form, with matter being the material used and the form the accompanying words and actions. The third element is an authorized minister to administer the sacrament.

All Christians use sacraments. The Protestants claim to use only two: baptism and the Eucharist, while Catholics claim to have seven sacraments: baptism, confirmation, confession, Eucharist, matrimony, holy orders and unction of the sick. In fact, there are more sacraments used by all Christians regardless of their denominations. They may not use the word sacrament, or they may use the word ordinance or no name at all. Dedication of a baby is very common among Protestants, especially among those who do not baptize their babies. Dedication is a sacrament because it confers inward grace by the power of the Holy Spirit through an outward sign and so is the assembling of Christians for their service regardless of what shape or form the service takes. It is the sacrament of unity. Many Christians are unaware of this even though they participate and are affected by it. When the congregation is assembled as a holy people to worship God, the individual member is affected by it according to his or her actual participation.
Matter plays an important role in the sacraments. They are not just symbols but are energized with grace—supernaturalized. Jesus healed, fed and strengthened people

during His earthly ministry through humble elements (matter) like spittle, mud, bread, wine, oil, etc. He could have performed His miracles directly, but He preferred to use material things (matter) to bestow His grace.

1. Baptism

Christ gave His command to baptize universally to the Apostles:
> Full authority has been given to me both in heaven and on earth; go therefore, and make disciples of all the nations. Baptize them in the name of the Father, and of the Son, and of the Holy Spirit! Teach them to carry out everything I have commanded you. And know that I am with you always until the end of the world! (Matthew 28:18–20 NIV paraphrased).

"Through baptism we are formed in the likeness and image of Jesus Christ. It was in one Spirit that all of us, whether Jews or Greek, slave or free, were baptized into one body" (1 Corinthians 12:13 NIV paraphrased). In baptism, a union with Christ's death and resurrection is not only symbolized but also brought about in reality.

Water is the main matter used in conjunction with this life-giving pronouncement: "I baptize you in the name of the Father, and of the Son, and of the Holy Spirit" (Catholic Catechism, 1997, article 1240). It is coupled with an action; either *immersion*, lowering of the body into the water; *aspersion* sprinkling of the water; or *infusion*, pouring of the water. Baptism was the normal conclusion of the apostolic preaching and teaching.

2. Confirmation or Baptism of the Holy Spirit

Catholics and Protestants differ in the way they confer this sacrament.

The Protestant Way

The person must love Jesus. The proof of that love is obedience to what He commands. "If you love me, you will obey what I command. And I will ask the Father, and he will give you another Counselor to be with you forever—the Spirit of truth" (John 14:15–17 NIV).

"We are witnesses of these things, and so is the Holy Spirit, whom God has given to those who obey Him" (Acts 5:32 NIV).

When these two conditions are fulfilled, nothing stands in the way for you to receive the Holy Spirit. All you have to do is ask your heavenly Father.

The Holy Spirit is a gift. "And you will receive the gift of the Holy Spirit. The promise is for you and your children and for all who are far off—for all whom the Lord our God will call" (Acts 2:38–39 NIV).

The giving of the Holy Spirit to a person is a sign of acceptance by God of that person. "God who knows the heart, showed that he accepted them by giving the Holy Spirit to them, just as he did to us" (Acts 15:8 NIV).
"I [John the Baptist] baptize you with water, but he [Jesus] will baptize you with the Holy Spirit" (Mark 1:8 NIV).

It is Jesus who baptizes you with the Holy Spirit. You ask the Father, and Jesus will, by the laying on of hands, baptize you with the Holy Spirit, through His established spiritual authority in your area or your surroundings. That authority may be your local pastor, a visiting evangelist or any Spirit-filled believer. A believer who does not know the Holy Spirit cannot give what he himself does not have. God is not restricted in His ways as to how to give the Holy Spirit. At times blowing or breathing on a person has the same results.

"Then Peter and John placed their hands on them, and they received the Holy Spirit" (Acts 8:17 NIV).

"Again Jesus said, 'Peace be with you! As the Father has sent me, I am sending you.' And with that He breathed on them and said, 'Receive the Holy Spirit' (John 20:21–22 NIV).

To baptize means to dip, to plunge or to immerse. In regards to baptizing with the Holy Spirit it means to pour out or to pour over. So the Holy Spirit is poured on or poured over a person.

The Catholic Way
The Holy Spirit is given to a baptized believer by anointing him or her with chrism (a sanctified mixture of oil and balsam) in the form of a cross on the forehead, the imposition of hands and saying the words, "[Name], receive the seal of the Holy Spirit, the Gift of the Father."

Regardless which way is chosen, the effects are tremendous. The confirmed person receives the Holy Spirit in a special way, and from then on he or she does well to have a close relationship with the Holy Spirit. The gifts of the Holy Spirit are also given, at least some of the gifts. Unfortunately most people neglect the Holy Spirit and very few operate in the gifts of the Holy Spirit. A great boldness to evangelize and to profess one's faith is a sure sign of the Holy Spirit's divine influence. The bishop is the ordinary minister of confirmation, or there can be an extraordinary minister, a priest for instance, to whom the power has been granted by office or by apostolic indult as an exception.

3. The Sacrament of Reconciliation or Confession

Once a person is born of God he or she is no longer a sinner. He or she is a new creation; the sinful nature has passed away. Nevertheless, many preachers keep on hammering into their flock the notion that they are sinners and that they deserve eternal punishment. You are what you think you are. If you think that you are a hopeless sinner, then you keep on sinning and sinning. But if you think you are a child of God in His image and likeness, you sin less and less until sin has absolutely no more hold on you. If you bark like a dog, that does not make you a dog, and if you sin as a born-of-God believer, that does not make you a sinner either.

Jesus knew what the human race is faced with, so He instituted the sacrament of reconciliation. Martin Luther introduced the notion that no man can forgive sin, therefore we ought to go directly to God, to Jesus, for the forgiveness of sins. That notion is flawed since Jesus handed over to mankind the authority on earth. Of course, we ask God to forgive us as soon as we realize our shortcomings, but that does not dispense us from seeking forgiveness in the sacrament of reconciliation.
Jesus gave His Apostles power and authority to reconcile us to the Father. They received Jesus' own power to forgive sins when He breathed on them and said, " Receive the Holy Spirit. If you forgive anyone his sins, they are forgiven; if you do not forgive them, they are not forgiven" (John 20: 22–23 NIV).

Jesus truly instituted the sacrament of reconciliation. The matter is sin. What is sin? Sin is the transgression of a natural or spiritual law or both put into place by God Himself. The form is the words of absolution in the form of the sign of the cross by the priest who administers the sacrament.

A sacrament is always given, that is divine influence is bestowed upon the recipient. For a sacrament to be valid, the minister has to abide by the form, words and actions that constitute the sacrament regardless of the minister's inner state. The recipient's inner state is crucial for the sacrament to be effective and valid. He must come with a sincere heart and be resolute not to sin willfully anymore and to change his ways to avoid temptations in the future. By confessing to a priest or minister, we know that we are forgiven and we receive grace to help us resist future temptations.

The Protestants have abolished confession to a minister but retained the counseling for their members. The Catholics get their counseling each time they go to confession. It is part of the renewal and purification of the believer, and each time divine grace is released to them. The Early Church called it the sacrament of reconciliation: second baptism, where the water is replaced with tears of repentance.

4. The Eucharist

One cannot separate the Eucharist from the Celebration of the Eucharist, which is the Holy Sacrifice of the Mass.

The Celebration of the Eucharist

The word Mass is derived from the Latin word *Missio,* meaning dismissed or sent out. "Go into all the world and preach the good news to all creation" (Mark 16:15 NIV).

The Mass comprises five parts:
1. Introductory Rite
2. The Liturgy of the Word: Scripture reading, preaching and profession of faith.
3. The Liturgy of the Eucharist: offering, consecration of bread and wine.
4. The Communion Rite: consuming the body and blood of Jesus Christ.
5. The Concluding Rite: dismissal and sending out.

Vatican II teaches the following:

> For all their (laity's) works, prayers, and apostolic endeavors, their ordinary married and family life, their daily labor, their mental and physical relaxation, if carried out in the Spirit, and even the hardships of life, if patiently borne—all of these become spiritual sacrifices acceptable through Jesus Christ. During the Celebration of the Eucharist, these sacrifices are most lovingly offered to the Father

along with the Lord's body. The faithful offer the divine Victim to
God and offer themselves along with it (Broderick, 1987, p. 198).

"You also, like living stones, are being built into a spiritual house to be a holy priesthood, offering spiritual sacrifices acceptable to God through Jesus Christ" (1 Peter 2:5 NIV).

"But you are a chosen people, a royal priesthood, a holy nation, a people belonging to God" (1 Peter 2:9 NIV).

The Eucharist as sacramental sacrifice is the Mass, wherein the body and blood of Christ, the same offering that took place on the cross at the crucifixion of Christ, become the sacrifice of the church because Christ unites the church's offering to his own. Through this offering and sacrifice, the efficacious sign of the consecration of the bread and wine, the sacrifice of the cross becomes present in a sacramental manner.

The Catholic Church teaches that the sacrifice of Christ on the cross occurred once for all. It cannot be repeated. Christ does not die again during Mass, but the same sacrifice that occurred on Calvary is made present at the altar. That's why the Mass is not another sacrifice but a participation in the same, once-for-all sacrifice.

The Sacrament of the Eucharist
The Catholic Church believes that in the Holy Eucharist the body, blood, spirit and divinity of Christ, the God-Man, are truly and substantially present under the appearances of bread and wine. This presence of the entire Christ is by reason of the transubstantiation of the bread and wine into the body and blood of Christ, which is accomplished in the unbloody sacrifice of the Mass. Jesus Himself instituted the Eucharist and requested its repetition (Luke 22:19–20).

The sacrament of the Eucharist is a true sacrifice, a representation of the sacrifice of Christ on the cross, for the ritual elements of the sacrifice are identical with the body and blood of Christ (Hebrews 9:12,14).

The Eucharist is a sacrament of unity. It is meant to unite the faithful more closely each day with God and with one another.

When a priest pronounces the words of Eucharistic consecration, the underlying reality of bread and wine is changed into the body and blood of Christ, given to us in sacrifice. That change has been given the name of 'transubstantiation'. This means that Christ Himself, true God and true Man, is really and substantially present, in a mysterious way, under the appearances of bread and wine.

The sacrifice of the Mass is not merely a ritual that commemorates a past sacrifice. In it, through the ministry of priests, Christ perpetuates the sacrifice of the cross in an unbloody manner. At the same time, the Eucharist is a meal that recalls the Last Supper, celebrates our unity together in Christ and anticipates the messianic banquet of the kingdom. In the Eucharist, Jesus nourishes Christians with His own self, the Bread of Life, so that they may become a people more acceptable to God and filled with greater love of God and others.

> Jesus said to them, "I tell you the truth, unless you eat the flesh of the Son of Man and drink his blood, you have no life in you. Whoever eats my flesh and drinks my blood has eternal life, and I will raise him up at the last day. For my flesh is real food and my blood is real drink. Whoever eats my flesh and drinks my blood remains in me, and I in him" (John 6:53–56 NIV).

Most Protestant denominations do not celebrate the Eucharist as mass. They took, however, one of the main three parts from it, so that their services are centered around that part: the Liturgy of the Word. From the Liturgy of the Eucharist, they retained the money offering, the tithe. Luther's theory called consubstantiation, the existence of God's presence in the Eucharist, was that the body and blood of Jesus Christ coexisted with the substances of bread and wine. Again, it is in strong contrast to the Catholic view of transubstantiation, that the sacramental bread and wine change into the body and blood of Jesus Christ when consecrated during the mass. Many Protestants, while taking communion, declare that they take the symbols of His body and blood: bread and wine. Jesus' words, in Matthew 26:26–28, clear the controversy.

> While they were eating, Jesus took bread, gave thanks and broke it, and gave it to his disciples, saying, "Take and eat; this is my body."
> Then he took the cup, gave thanks and offered it to them, saying, "Drink from it, all of you. This is my blood of the covenant, which is poured out for many for the forgiveness of sins." (NIV).

Jesus did not say, "This is the symbol of my body" nor "the symbol of my blood," but "this is my body … this is my blood." It is the spiritual, which is unseen, manifested in the natural, material, which is seen.

The Eucharist is the sacrament of love, the love Jesus Christ has for all humanity. It is represented by His Sacred Heart. The worship and reparation to Christ for men's ingratitude, manifested particularly by indifference to the Holy Eucharist, is directed to the person of Jesus Christ Himself.

Our Lord Jesus appeared to St. Margaret Mary Alacoque at the Visitation Convent of Paray-le-Monial (France) in 1673. Jesus gave St. Margaret twelve promises for all those who promote the worship to Him by displaying in their home a representation of His love, a picture of His Sacred Heart. The promises are as follows:

1. I will give them all the graces necessary in their state of life.
2. I will establish peace in their homes.
3. I will comfort them in all their afflictions.
4. I will be their secure refuge during life and above all, in death.
5. I will bestow abundant blessings on all their undertakings.
6. Sinners will find in my Heart the source and the infinite ocean of mercy.
7. By devotion to my Heart, lukewarm souls shall grow fervent.
8. Fervent souls shall rise quickly to high perfection.
9. I will bless every place where a picture of my Heart shall be set up and honored.
10. I will give to priests the gift of touching the most hardened hearts.
11. Those who promote this devotion shall have their names written in my Heart, never to be blotted out.
12. I will grant the grace of final penitence to those who communicate (receive Holy Communion) on the first Friday of nine consecutive months.

5. Matrimony

Marriage involves three parties: the bride, the groom, and God. When two Christians receive the sacrament of matrimony, God is with them, witnessing and blessing their marriage covenant, which is permanent and only death of either spouse can break. This holy union of husband and wife is a living symbol of the loving relationship between Christ and the church.

> Wives, submit to your husband as to the Lord. For the husband is the head of the wife as Christ is the head of the church,

his body, of which he is the Savior. Now as the church submits to Christ, so also wives should submit to their husbands in everything.

Husbands, love your wives, just as Christ loved the church and gave himself up for her to make her holy, cleansing her by the washing with water through the word, and to present her to himself as a radiant church, without stain or wrinkle or any other blemish, but holy and blameless. In the same way, husbands ought to love their wives as their own bodies" (Ephesians 5:22–28 NIV).

The marriage covenant is made by two persons of the opposite sex by which each acquires the exclusive and irrevocable right over their bodies for the procreation and education of children. Marriage can only take place between two persons of the opposite sex. So-called gay marriage is an impossibility—not a marriage at all but an abomination to God and all mankind. There is a uniqueness in the consecration of husband and wife over parenthood. Gay couples adopting children should be banned by any government and church.

Vatican II declared, "Firmly established by the Lord, the unity of marriage will radiate from the equal personal dignity of wife and husband, a dignity acknowledged by mutual and total love" (Broderick, 1987, p. 372). There is great freedom in how to celebrate the sacrament of marriage. However, certain aspects should be stressed like the liturgy of the Word, which shows the importance of Christian marriage, the duties and responsibilities towards each other and the children, the free consent, the nuptial blessing and the reception of the Holy Eucharist.

6. Holy Orders

God calls men and woman to a special priestly ministry. Holy Orders is the sacrament through which these men and woman receive spiritual power and the necessary grace to serve the church in the capacity of deacons, priests and bishops. They serve as pastors, teachers and spiritual fathers who heal, feed and strengthen God's people but most importantly through preaching and the administration of the sacraments. The priest must serve as a teacher as Christ Himself was and is; serve as Christ the priest, to unite and offer up the spiritual sacrifices of the faithful to the Eucharistic sacrifice; and serve as Christ the pastor, to bring the faithful together in unity and to nurture them to maturity.

The Rite of Holy Orders

The Rite of Holy Orders consists of the following steps:

1. The choosing of the candidates.
2. The consent by the entire priestly people.
3. The instruction of the candidates by the bishop.
4. The affirmation of the candidates' willingness to celebrate the mysteries of Christ.
5. The candidates make a promise of obedience to the bishop and his successors.
6. The bishop invokes the Holy Spirit upon those to be ordained.
7. The laying on of hands by the bishop, which is the actual conferring of the sacrament. Then in turn, all priests present lay their hands on each candidate.
8. The prayer of consecration.
9. The investiture: the stole, a sign of priestly power in Christ.
10. The palms of the hands of each new priest are anointed with chrism.
11. The paten (bread) and the chalice (wine) is offered to each new priest
12. The kiss of peace

The liturgy of the Eucharist follows. The newly ordained concelebrate Mass with the bishop.

The laying on of hands is used not only to give the Holy Spirit but also to confer authority and spiritual power. "For this reason, I remind you to fan into flame the gift of God, which is in you through the laying on of my hands" (2 Timothy 1:6 NIV).

"They presented these men to the apostles, who prayed and laid their hands on them" (Acts 6:6 NIV). Priests are demanded to acquire a great personal spiritual life (Phase One to be successful in Phase Two), to undergo a program of ongoing training and learning and to have a cultured competency that enables them to work in a variety of societal environments.

Unfortunately, Martin Luther got rid of the priesthood. Most Protestant ministers are not ordained priests according to the order of Melchizedek. The only manner shown by Melchizedek was the use of bread and wine. A priest sacrifices the items offered—that is the main task of all priests, in all cultures at all time.

The Priesthood of the Faithful

"But you are a chosen people, a royal priesthood, a holy nation, a people belonging to God" (1 Peter 2:9 NIV).

As a redeemed people they are united to the kingdom through the priesthood and the redemptive act of sacrifice offered by Christ for all.

> To him who loves us and has freed us from our sins by his blood, and has made us to be a kingdom and priests to serve his God and Father—to him be glory and power for ever and ever! Amen" (Revelation 1:5–6 NIV).

"You have made them to be a kingdom and priests to serve our God, and they will reign on the earth" (Revelation 5:10 NIV).

In the celebration of the Eucharist, they offer themselves with Christ's sacrifice through the Holy Spirit to their heavenly Father. "Therefore, I urge you, brothers, in view of God's mercy, to offer your bodies as living sacrifices, holy and pleasing to God—this is your spiritual act of worship" (Romans 12:1 NIV).

"Through Jesus, therefore, let us continually offer to God a sacrifice of praise—the fruit of lips that confess his name. [Phase One] And do not forget to do good and to share with others, for with such sacrifices God is pleased" [Phase Two] (Hebrews 13:15–16 NIV). God made us a kingdom and priests to share in His kingdom and in His priesthood.

7. The Anointing of the Sick

The anointing of the sick differs from the gift of healing, which is one of the gifts of the Holy Spirit. Any priest or minister can confer the sacrament of the anointing of the sick, but only those who have and operate in the gift of healing can provide healing through the gift. The result is, however, the same.

One of my uncles was dying of a serious illness and was also quite advanced in age. After receiving the sacrament of the anointing of the sick, he not only totally recovered but also went back to work as a tree feller and lived many more years.

I myself was healed of lung cancer but not by the sacrament. In the middle of the night, I got up and asked Jesus to do something about it. I was healed instantly. Another time, the pastor called out the sickness, and the illness was healed. When he mentioned, "rib" my broken rib also was instantly healed.

The matter of the sacrament is olive oil or if necessary any vegetable oil properly blessed by a bishop or priest. One single anointing on the forehead or any other part of the body suffices. The form is as follows:

> Through this holy anointing and His most loving mercy, may the Lord assist you by the grace of the Holy Spirit so that, when you have been freed from your sins, He may save you and in His goodness raise you up (Broderick, p. 40).

The sacrament of the anointing of the sick was instituted by Christ our Lord as a true and proper sacrament of the New Testament. When Jesus sent out the twelve disciples to preach, "They drove out many demons, and anointed with oil many that were sick and healed them" (Mark 6:13 NIV).

And James tells us in his epistle:

> Is any one of you sick? He should call the elders of the church to pray over him and anoint him with oil in the name of the Lord. And the prayer offered in faith will make the sick person well; the Lord will raise him up. If he has sinned, he will be forgiven" (James 5:14–15 NIV).

The effects of this sacrament are manifold. It unites the sick person to the passion of Christ, for his own good and that of the whole church; it gives strength, peace and courage to endure in a Christian manner the sufferings of illness; and it provides forgiveness of sins and the restoration of health. The restoration of health does not always happen. There can be hindrances like unforgiveness, bitterness or a lack of faith of the person involved or a lack of faith of those being present. But many times, there are people with great faith, mature Christians who are not being restored to health. In fact, many die with their illness. What's the answer? We find the answer in the sacrament of the baptism of blood.

8. The Baptism of Blood

The Bible mentions three baptisms: the baptism of water, the baptism of the Holy Spirit and the baptism of blood. The baptism of water you receive at the time you are born of God; by your asking, receiving and accepting Jesus Christ (Christ in you, His responsibility) and through the baptism you are baptized into Christ (you in Christ, your responsibility). "You are all sons of God through faith in Christ Jesus, for all of you who were baptized into Christ have clothed yourselves with Christ"

(Galatians 3:26–27 NIV). The baptism of the Holy Spirit should be received after that.These two baptisms are right at the start of your Christian life and walk, but the baptism of blood may occur at any time of your life, or it may not occur at all. The baptism of blood is the least known and is often misunderstood or not understood at all.

There are two distinct aspects of the baptism of blood, having to do with the respective recipients. One category is for those who give their lives for Jesus Christ rather than apostatize and deny Him. It is the sacrifice of one's life. Many became martyrs during the persecutions, and many become martyrs today. They may be Christians, or they may be like the thief on the cross and give their lives at the last moment for Christ and be saved through the baptism of blood, martyrdom for Christ.

The other category is for those who live their lives as living testaments of the faith but die of natural causes. They are exclusively Christians. Martyrdom is an exceptional gift and the perfect proof of love. Martyrdom may be applied to those who die at the hands of persecutors or to those who die slowly at the hands of circumstances in the service of Jesus Christ for others. Laying down one's life for Christ and others is the ultimate sacrifice and gift one can make. "For God so loved the world that he gave his one and only Son, that whoever believes in him shall not perish but have eternal life" (John 3:16 NIV).

"Greater love has no one than this, that he lay down his life for his friends" (John 15:13 NIV).

The blood baptism has to do with dying literally and suffering. The human nature is opposed to dying and to suffering, so it is not something very popular or something to look forward to. All death and suffering have their origin in the fall of Adam and Eve. It is a negative, but even from a negative, God can make a positive. Jesus Christ through His passion, death and resurrection brought salvation to the human race, and so through our death and suffering He can bring that salvation to people.

Many Christians entertain the notion that since Christ suffered for us, so we do not have to suffer. In fact, I have never met anyone who did not suffer one way or another. Those people base their understanding on the following verse. "He carried our infirmities and bore our diseases" (Matthew 8:17 NIV paraphrased). This verse does not say that we will have no infirmities or diseases; it simply means that our infirmities and diseases are not in vain like those of the unbelievers. The believers do not suffer in vain.

"And by his wounds we are healed" (Isaiah 53:5 NIV). You cannot be healed unless you are sick in the first place. After being sick we have at our disposition healing purchased for us by Jesus Christ through His wounds.

Why do we suffer?
Originally suffering entered the human race through the fall of Adam and Eve. Suffering is not something God created or God put on people. At best God allows suffering, but He not only allows suffering, He also turns it into something creative, positive and good. We may suffer for many reasons. We may suffer for the gospel.

> Blessed are you who when people insult you, persecute you and falsely say all kind of evil against you because of me. Rejoice and be glad, because great is your reward in heaven, for in the same way they persecuted the prophets who where before you" (Matthew 5:11–12.NIV).

We suffer because of our shortcomings and faults. Sickness and disease are often brought on by our faulty living habits. We also suffer because of others, which is hard to accept and hard to forgive.

How should a Christian suffer?
Since we all suffer at one time or another, let's look at Jesus—how He suffered. Jesus used suffering, death and His resurrection to bring redemption and salvation to the human race. He looked forward to His passion and death not for suffering's sake but for the glory it would bring to the human race.

"I have come to bring fire on the earth, and how I wish it were already kindled! But I have a baptism to undergo, and how distressed I am until it is completed" (Luke 12:49–50 NIV).

"I have come to bring fire to the earth, and how I wish it were blazing already. There is a baptism I must still receive, and what constraint I am under until it is completed!" (Luke 12:49–50 NJB). Jesus was distressed and under great constraint to see it happen. It was something He had to do, to undergo, He came to earth for it.

When Peter the Apostle tried to prevent Jesus from receiving the baptism of blood, he received the greatest rebuke.

> He than began to teach them that the Son of Man must suffer many things and be rejected by the elders, chief priests and teachers of the law, and that he must be killed and after three days rise again. He spoke plainly about this, and Peter took him aside and began to rebuke him.
>
> But when Jesus turned and looked at his disciples, he rebuked Peter, "Get behind me, Satan!" he said. "You do not have in mind the things of God, but the things of men" (Mark 8:31–33 NIV).

Even though Jesus looked forward to His passion, at the time it really happened, He was troubled to death and asked His Father to take this cup away from Him.

> He took Peter, James and John along with him, and he began to be deeply distressed and troubled. "My soul is overwhelmed with sorrow to the point of death," he said to them. "Stay here and keep watch."
>
> Going a little farther, he fell to the ground and prayed that if possible the hour might pass from him. "Abba, Father," he said, " everything is possible for you. Take this cup from me. Yet not what I will, but what you will" (Mark 14:33–36 NIV).

Some people may say, "That's for Jesus not for us."

> Then James and John, the sons of Zebedee, came to him, "Teacher," they said, "we want you to do for us whatever we ask."
>
> "What do you want me to do for you?" he asked.
>
> They replied, "Let one of us sit at your right and the other at your left in your glory."
>
> "You do not know what you are asking, "Jesus said. "Can you drink the cup I drink or be baptized with the baptism I am baptized with?"
>
> "We can," they answered.
>
> Jesus said to them, " You will drink the cup I drink and be baptized with the baptism I am baptized with, but to sit at my right or left is not for me to grant. These places belong to those for whom they have been prepared (Mark 10:35–40 NIV)

James and John, the sons of Zebedee, two of Jesus' disciples were baptized with the baptism Jesus was baptized with, the baptism of blood. There are many disciples of Jesus both then and now who were and are baptized with the baptism of blood. It is a great privilege and honor. Most of those baptized with the baptism of blood are martyrs not by choice but by circumstances. There is, however, a very small group who are baptized by choice. Their love for God is so great, their likeness in the image of God so profound, that they are given by God through grace (divine influence) the stigmata. Stigmata comes from a Greek word meaning marks. It refers to the wounds that appear on the flesh of individuals, either all the wounds or some, visible or invisible, but painful—at different times and seasons more painful. These wounds correspond to the wounds suffered by Jesus Christ at the crucifixion. There are more than 300 well-documented cases worldwide. St. Catherine of Sienna requested from our Lord that the stigmata be invisible, not evident on her body. A most recent person with the stigmata was Padre Pio, an Italian Catholic monk. I personally wrote him a letter, and he responded. He also operated in the gifts of the Holy Spirit and often revealed in the confessional the penitent's hidden shortcomings and sins. Are there any Bible examples of persons who bore the stigmata? Yes, Paul the Apostle. "Finally, let no one cause me trouble, for I bear on my body the marks [stigmata] of Jesus" (Galatians 6:17 NIV). They were not spiritual or invisible wounds but visible because Paul says, "on my body."

Some people think that suffering is controversial but not so according to the Scriptures.

> Dear friends do not be surprised at the painful trial you are suffering, as though something strange were happening to you. But rejoice that you participate in the sufferings of Christ, so that you may be overjoyed when his glory is revealed (1 Peter 4:12–13 NIV).

"So then, those who suffer according to God's will should commit themselves to their faithful Creator and continue to do good" (1 Peter 4:19 NIV).

"Now I rejoice in what was suffered for you, and I fill up in my flesh what is still lacking in regard to Christ's afflictions, for the sake of his body, which is the church" (Colossians 1:24 NIV).

> Now if we are children, then we are heirs—heirs of God and co-heirs with Christ, if indeed we share in his suffering in order that we may also share in his glory. I consider that our present sufferings are

not worth comparing with the glory that will be revealed in us (Romans 8:17–18 NIV).

"For it has been granted to you on behalf of Christ not only to believe in him, but also to suffer for him, since you are going through the same struggle you saw I had, and now hear that I still have" (Philippians 1:29–30 NIV).

"I want to know Christ and the power of his resurrection and the fellowship of sharing in his suffering, becoming like him in his death, and so, somehow, to attain to the resurrection from the dead" (Philippians 3:10–11 NIV).

"To this you were called, because Christ suffered for you, leaving you an example, that you should follow in his steps" (1 Peter 2:21 NIV).

"It is better, if it is God's will, to suffer for doing good than for doing evil" (1 Peter 3:17 NIV).

"Therefore, since Christ suffered in his body, arm yourselves also with the same attitude, because he who has suffered in his body is done with sin" (1 Peter 4:1 NIV).

These Bible verses clearly indicate how a Christian should conduct himself when faced with suffering:
- "Participate in the suffering of Christ" (1 Peter 4:12-13).
- "According to the will of God." (1 Peter 4:19).
- "To supplement what is lacking to the body of Christ" (Colossians 1:24).
- "Share in Christ's suffering" (Romans 8:17-18).
- "Suffer for him" (Philippians 1:29-30).
- "Fellowship in his suffering" (Philippians 3:10-11).
- "To follow in his footsteps" (1 Peter 2:21).
- "Trust in him, commit yourself to him" (1 Peter 4:19).
- "While you suffer, continue to do good" (1 Peter 4:19).

The disciple is not above the master. We all suffer, but not all are candidates for the baptism of blood. Candidates are sons of God. They become the seed for a great harvest of souls. "I tell you the truth, unless a kernel of wheat falls to the ground and dies, it remains only a single seed. But if it dies, it produces many seeds" (John 12:24 NIV).

Who are sons of God? Those who are led by the Holy Spirit, the peacekeepers and those who love their enemies. "You are all sons of God through faith in Christ Jesus" (Galatians 3:26 NIV).

"..because those who are led by the Spirit of God are sons of God" (Romans 8:14 NIV).

"Blessed are the peacemakers for they will be called sons of God" (Matthew 5:9 NIV).

"...love your enemies and pray for those who persecute you, that you may be sons of your Father in heaven" (Matthew 5:45 NIV).

Only sons of God are priesthood. The primary function of the priests is worship offered up by the Holy Spirit through Jesus Christ to the Father. "For all their (laity's) works, prayers, and apostolic endeavors, their ordinary married and family life, their daily labor, their mental and physical relaxation, if carried out in the Spirit, and even the hardships of life, if patiently borne—all of these become spiritual sacrifices acceptable through Jesus Christ. During the Celebration of the Eucharist, these sacrifices are most lovingly offered to the Father along with the Lord's body. The faithful offer the divine Victim to God and offer themselves along with it" (Broderick, 1987, p. 198).

"You also, like living stones, are being built into a spiritual house to be a holy priesthood, offering spiritual sacrifices acceptable to God through Jesus Christ" (1 Peter 2:5 NIV).
"But you are a chosen people, a royal priesthood, a holy nation, a people belonging to God"(1 Peter 2:9 NIV).

The Eucharist is celebrated on a continual basis because of time zones. So at any time, the sons of God, the royal priesthood, can offer up together with the sacrifice of Jesus Christ everything which makes up their life—the physical, mental and spiritual suffering, all good things and all bad things. You may wonder how exactly; here is how.

Very few people are taught how they should use the mind. We take it for granted that everybody knows how to think properly, and we do not realize that all our thought processes are governed by specific principles common to all human beings. Scriptures declare, "My people perish for lack of knowledge." (Hosea 4:6 paraphrased NIV). Even those who get the knowledge, very few know how to process it properly.

Everything that happens to us, everything that is said to us and everything that we sense with our senses can be regarded as influence having an affect on us. We are constantly bombarded with influence, good and bad. It is clear if we do not know how to process that influence, we are not functioning properly, and a lot of that influence is wasted but not only wasted; it becomes detrimental to us and eventually may even destroy us. We will not live our life to its full potential physically, mentally and spiritually. To know more about how your mind works refer to Appendix A.

9. The Sacrament of Dedication

Dedication of infants to the Lord is much more prevalent among Protestants than Catholics. It is nevertheless a sacrament: an outward sign to confer inward grace by the power of the Holy Spirit.
The Protestants who object to infant baptism feel some kind of guilt. To appease that guilt they often rely on dedicating their infants to God. "So now I give him to the Lord. For his whole life he will be given over to the Lord" (1 Samuel 1:28 NIV). Here we see Hannah dedicating her son to the Lord.

> And when the day came for them to be purified in keeping with the
> Law of Moses, they took him up to Jerusalem to present him to the
> Lord—observing what is written in the Law of the Lord: *Every first-*
> *born male must be consecrated to the Lord* (Luke 2:22–23 NJB).

Only the mother had to be purified, but Jesus was dedicated to the Lord. Dedication is a very noble thing to do, but it does not replace baptism. The same argument the Protestants use in not baptizing their infants holds true in dedication. In each case, the will of the infant is put aside and ignored, and the faith of the infant does not come into play at all. A conscious decision for Christ on the part of the baby is absent.

A much better way is to baptize the infants and then present and dedicate them to God Almighty. Nevertheless, once infants reach the age of reason, they should and must seal that dedication by their own acceptance.

10. The Sacrament of Unity

The sacrament of unity is given each time two or three come together in Jesus' name and during the assembling of Christians for their worship service, regardless of what shape or form the service takes, under the guidance of the Holy Spirit. Many Christians are unaware of this sacrament even though they participate in it and are affected by it. When the congregation is assembled as a holy people to worship God, the individual member is affected by it according to his or her actual participation. "For where two or three come together in my name, there I am with them" (Matthew 18:20 NIV). That's the time to ask God for anything according to His will, and He promised us it would be given to us.

The sacrament of unity is one of the most powerful sacraments. "So that they may be one, as we are one" (John 17:11 NIV). It is a unity of relationship, an intimate union with God and all mankind. In the upper room at Pentecost, that unity marked the coming of the Holy Spirit and the beginning of the church. "They were all together in one place" (Acts 2:1 NIV).

"They all joined together constantly in prayer" (Acts 1:14 NIV).

The greatest outpouring of the Holy Spirit will happen when all Christians, of all denominations, come together in unity of relationship in the name of Jesus Christ. All Christians are children of God, but not all are sons and daughters of God. The peacemakers among the denominations are sons and daughters of God. "Blessed are the peacemakers for they will be called sons of God" (Matthew 5:9 NIV).
These ten sacraments are the most common ones. But God is in no way restricted from using other means, other sacraments, to dispense His grace to divinely influence the human race as a whole or the individual members of His body. It is up to the individual to receive and accept His grace regardless of the means, the sacrament that God chooses to use at a particular time.

7. The Christian Family

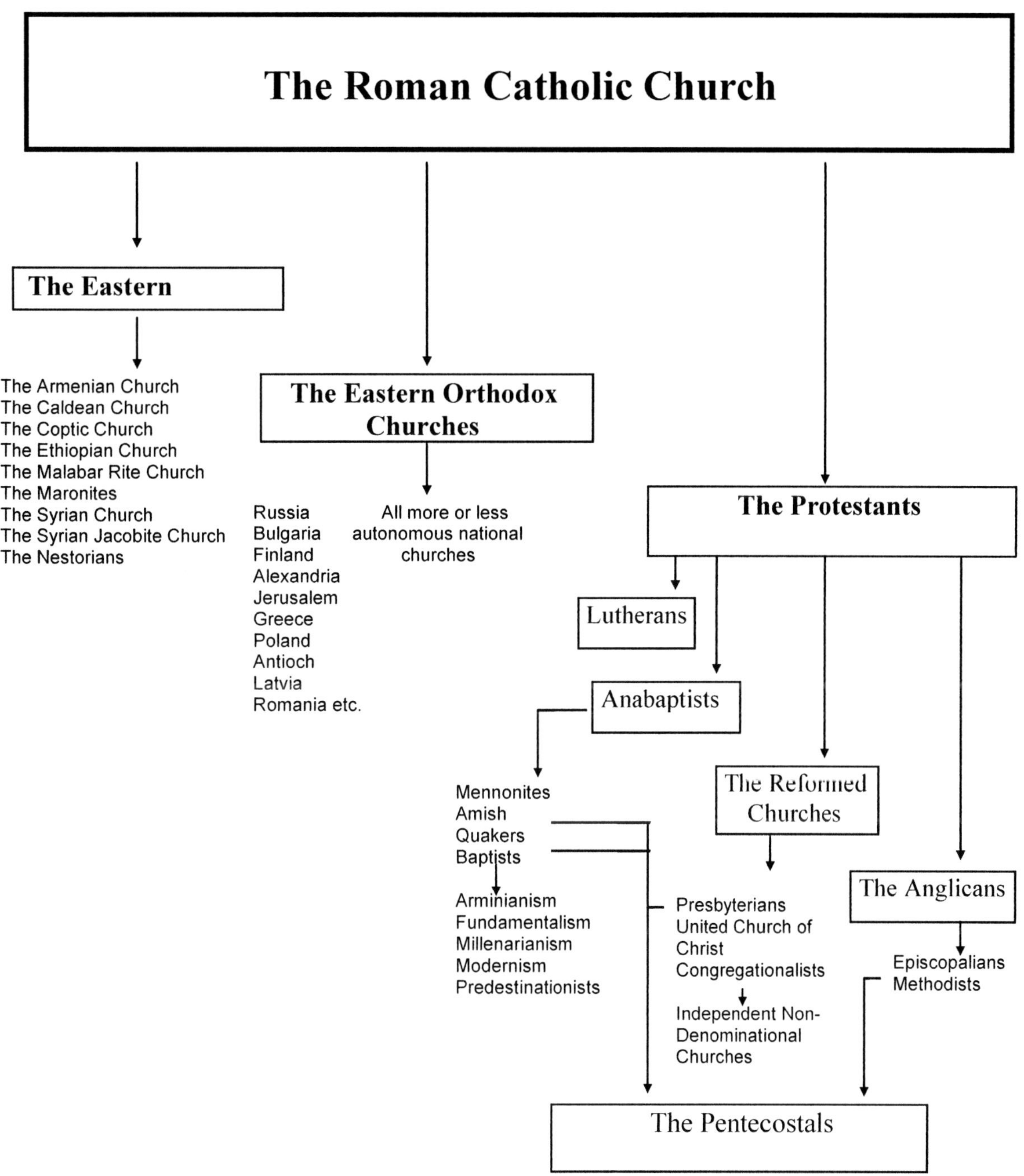

> "I am the good shepherd; I know my sheep and my sheep know
> me—just as the Father knows me and I know the Father—and I lay
> down my life for the sheep. I have other sheep that are not of this
> sheep pen. I must bring them also. They too listen to my voice, and
> there shall be one flock and one shepherd" (John 10:14–16 NIV).

Unfortunately, the one flock is not yet a reality. We know, however, the sheep that will be part of the one flock Jesus is talking about. "This sheep pen" is the original church birthed at Pentecost. That church is what we know as the Roman Catholic Church.

The Roman Catholic Church

No other Christian denomination can lay claim to their origin in Jerusalem. It is the true church and it has proclaimed to this very day the true teaching and doctrine of Jesus Christ. All Catholic bishops and popes can have their lineage of predecessors traced back to the time of the apostles, something that is impossible in Protestant denominations of which most of them do not even have bishops. The Roman Catholic Church has well over one billion members and is growing rapidly. It is the mother church, the only church founded by Jesus Christ Himself. All other denominations are merely offshoots. As long as the doctrines of those offshoots adhere at least to dogmas of the creed, they too are part of the Christian family. The New Testament was written by early Roman Catholics of whom we well know their names: Matthew, Mark, John, Lukas, Paul, James and Jude. The Roman Catholic Church is a truly universal church; it is neither national nor ethnic and extends to every nation and race. Its members profess one belief system (one faith), profess one doctrine expressed in the creed, participate in the seven sacraments and are governed by the pope and bishops. The first offshoots from the Roman Catholic Church are the Eastern Christian Churches.

The Eastern Christian Churches

The Eastern Christian churches are divided into two groups: the Uniat churches and the dissident or schismatic churches. The Uniat churches are in communion with the Roman Catholic Church and acknowledge the supremacy of the pope but keep their own liturgy and organization. They teach the same faith and morals as the Roman Catholic Church.

The Armenian Church

In Armenia, the church was outstanding until 381 (the Council of Constantinople). Persia defeated Armenia in the seventh century and the Armenians opted for heresies. In 593 the church split with some still in communion with Rome and others who set up a new, dissident church. The rite of the Armenian Church is ancient Armenian and is used by the Uniat and the dissident churches. A small number (about 150,000) located mostly in Germany and the United States, still in communion with Rome, come under the jurisdiction of the local bishop. Their celebration of the Eucharist is called liturgy and follows mostly the Byzantine rite. Efforts for reconciliation have so far failed. Those separated from the Catholic Church are reputed to be Monophysites, claiming only one nature in Jesus Christ.

The Chaldean Church

The Chaldean Church follows the Chaldean rite also called the East Syrian, Assyrian, or Persian rite. It is a liturgy of the Uniat East Syrian written in old Syriac. Communion is given by dipping a bit of consecrated bread into the chalice of consecrated wine.

The Coptic Church

Both the Catholic Coptic Church and the dissident Coptic Church follow the Coptic rite. The liturgical language is the early Egyptian (Coptic) along with Greek and Arabic. The dissident church follows the Monophysitic heresy and denies the supremacy of the pope. Their orders are valid; they administer the sacraments in a different manner, baptism for example by immersion. The Catholic Coptic Church was reconciled in the eighteenth century and under Pope Leo XIII, was given a patriarchate, which is located in Alexandria.

The Ethiopian Church

There are about five million Christian Ethiopians, descendants of those who migrated to Africa from Southern Arabia. They form the Ethiopian Church. When the Alexandrian Church fell into Monophysitism and formed the Coptic Church, Ethiopia fell into the same error. Through missionary work in the eighteenth and nineteenth centuries about one eighth of the Ethiopian Church has returned to Roman Catholic union. The rite of the Ethiopian Church is similar to the Roman rite.

The Malabar Rite Church

The Syro-Malabar rite is the liturgy used by the Eastern Catholics of Malabar of Southern India, in the state of Kerola. The Syriac language and much of the Syriac liturgy are used.

The Maronites

The members of the Eastern Catholic Church, who are Arabic-speaking Syrians inhabiting Lebanon are called Maronites. They are in communion with Rome and have a college for the education of their clergy in Rome. In the year 1181, at the time of the Crusades, all Maronite brethren, together with their bishops and patriarch of Lebanon, made peace with Rome and became attached to the Holy See.

The Syrian Church and the Syrian Jacobite Church

The Catholic Syrians use the Syrian rite. It is also used by the dissident church, the Jacobite Syrians. The Jacobite Church is a Monophysite Church, which Baradai began in 543. Jacob Baradai was a Monophysite monk, consecrated bishop of Edessa. Since 1500, a movement began to obtain a reunion with Rome, which continues to this day. The Jacobite patriarch has resided in Damascus since 1959 ruling over 11 dioceses: four in Syria, two in Iraq, two in Turkey, one in Lebanon, one in Jerusalem and one in Hackensack, New Jersey.

The Nestorians

An isolated part of Syria maintains a Nestorian diocese in Malabar. In 428, a priest by the name of Nestorius, started this heresy after he became the patriarch of Constantinople. He declared that the blessed Virgin Mary was mother only of Christ's human nature and he banned the term mother of God, he also taught that only Christ as man died on the cross. This heresy was condemned in 431 by the Council of Ephesus.

The Eastern Orthodox Churches

Right from the beginning, differences were present in the church when the gospel was preached in Rome and in Corinth. But the distinctive Eastern Christian faith appeared first under Constantine in 330. Constantine made Christendom lawful throughout the Roman Empire. He moved his capital to Byzantium, later named Constantinople, which is now known as Istanbul. A culture separate from Rome developed. He created an alliance between state and church. Constantinople became the home of the Eastern Christian tradition and the crossroad of the new Byzantine civilization. The history of Eastern Orthodoxy was shaped by the ever-present conflict between state and church. In 476, the Western Roman Empire collapsed but the eastern half continued under the title of the Byzantine Empire with its headquarters in Constantinople. The patriarch of Constantinople had jurisdiction over the patriarchates of Alexandria, Antioch and Jerusalem but served under the emperor. Many patriarchs were good and holy bishops who ruled well and resisted imperial encroachment on church matters, but it is difficult to withstand the designs of power-hungry and meddlesome emperors with armies at their disposal.

The first conflict arose when Emperor Constantine appointed an Arian heretic as patriarch. Pope Julius excommunicated the patriarch in 343, and Constantinople remained in schism until John Chrysostom became patriarch in 398.

Arianism was condemned as a heresy at the Council of Nicaea in 325. It took its name from Arius, a priest of Alexandria who was transient at Antioch. It taught that the Son of God is not of one nature or substance with the Father, nor equal to Him in dignity and not co-eternal.

Iconoclasm

The heresy of image breaking (iconoclasm) arose in the eighth century (787). It declared religious veneration of pictures and images unlawful. The heresy was fostered by the Paulicians, Jews, and Moslems and aided by the Eastern Emperors. At the second ecumenical Council of Nicaea, the church defined the distinction between adoration given to God and the veneration paid to saints and declared that such veneration is an act of homage not to the image or icon but to the person depicted.

Icon is the Greek word for image, painted or glazed on flat surfaces of wood or metal and used in Eastern Churches instead of statues. The icons play an important part in the liturgy of the Eastern Churches more so than the statues of the Roman rite. Icons are given to a child at birth, usually of his or her patron saint, also to newly married couples. The Orthodox believer, when entering the church, goes first to the iconostasis, the wall of paintings that separates the sanctuary from the nave. There he kisses the icons before taking his seat in the congregation. When an Orthodox visitor enters the home of his Orthodox host, he will greet the icons first by crossing himself and bowing. Only then will he greet his host. Normally, an icon is hanging in the eastern corner of the living room and bedroom. The iconoclastic conflict was a disagreement over the use of icons.

There is a question to be asked, "Do Catholics worship statues and Orthodox icons?" The answer is, of course, no. Ignorance and misunderstanding on the side of the accusers is to blame for such ridiculous claims. They base their accusations on Exodus 20:4–5. "You shall not make for yourself an idol in the form of anything in heaven above or on the earth beneath or in the waters below. You shall not bow down to them or worship them" (NIV).

The making and use of statues and icons depicting God and the saints is a thoroughly biblical practice. God said to make them. He even commanded it.

> And make two cherubim out of hammered gold at the end of the cover. Make one cherub on one end and the second cherub on the other; make the cherubim of one piece with the cover, at the two ends" (Exodus 25:18–19 NIV).

"The Lord said to Moses, 'Make a snake and put it up on a pole; anyone who is bitten can look at it and live'" (Numbers 21:8 NIV). In this case, a large bronze statue of the serpent healed the one who looked at it.

Catholics and Orthodox use statues and icons to recall the person or thing depicted. They are also used as teaching tools. God forbids the worship of images as gods but He does not ban the making of images, He even recommends it. The Holy Spirit revealed Himself under visible forms: a dove, tongues of fire etc. Protestants use these images when drawing or painting biblical episodes and when they wear Holy Spirit lapel pins or place dove emblems on their cars. God revealed Himself under a visible form in Jesus Christ. We can make representations of God. Protestants use a myriad of biblical representations on Bibles, T-shirts, bumper stickers, greeting cards, fish emblems, *icthus*, etc.

Statues and pictures of evil, demonic representations on various artifacts or art often bring demonic oppression and/or possession of the person wearing such objects or harboring them in their homes. Don't you think statues and pictures representing God and His saints will have a beneficial effect?

People are bowing and often kneeling in front of statues and icons. That does not mean they are worshipping the icon or the statue. We must not confuse the legitimate veneration of a sacred image with the sin of idolatry. In Japan, people show respect by bowing in greeting; that does not mean they are worshipping. It is the equivalent of the Western handshake.

It is not wrong for anyone to use statues and images of God and His saints to deepen his or her knowledge and love of God. Jesus Christ is the image of the invisible God, the firstborn of all creation. In other words, Christ is the tangible divine icon of the unseen, infinite God; we, the believers, are made in His image.

The Iconoclastic heresy, which sought to eliminate all sacred images, was fought by the pope and the Western bishops. The practice of venerating icons is still very much part of Orthodox liturgy and spirituality despite the fact that the patriarch of Constantinople sided with the heretical, iconoclastic emperor at that time.

In 987, the pagan prince Vladimir of Kiev looked to other nations for a new religion. He dispatched envoys to observe the practice of Judaism, Islam, Roman Catholicism and Eastern Orthodoxy. The worship service of the Greek Orthodox Church determined his choice. In time, Eastern Christianity became the faith of much of the Slavic world.

A number of events eventually led to the Great Schism between Eastern and Western Christendom. The Catholic Normans' conquest of Southern Italy was but the beginning. The Catholic Normans took over the Byzantine-Rite Greek communities and requested that they adopt the Latin-Rite custom of using unleavened bread for the Eucharist. That custom is based on 1 Corinthians 5:8. "Therefore let us keep the Festival, not with the old yeast, the yeast of malice and wickedness, but with bread without yeast, the bread of sincerity and truth" (NIV). This caused great aggravation among the Greek Catholics. In response, Patriarch Cerularius ordered all the Latin-Rite communities in Constantinople to use leavened bread for the Eucharist. The Latins refused, so the patriarch closed their churches.

In 1054, Pope Leo the IX sent a three-man delegation, headed by Cardinal Humbert, to visit Patriarch Cerularius in an attempt to straighten out the matter. Both sides managed to infuriate each other over diplomatic courtesies, so matters worsened.

In 1204, Christian knights of the Fourth Crusade sacked the principal city of Christendom, Constantinople. It never recovered its economical or military strength. In 1453, it fell to the Turks and Hagia Sophia; the major Orthodox Church in Constantinople became a Muslim mosque. The East's final break with Rome came in the 1450 through unresolved theological disputes along with the refusal of Orthodox prelates to acknowledge the authority of the pope. The result was the use of the Greek rather than the Latin language; also their doctrine was less explicitly defined.

The Catholic Church and the Orthodox Church have valid orders and apostolic succession through the episcopacy. Both celebrate the same sacraments, both believe almost exactly the same theology and both proclaim the same faith in Christ Jesus.

There are nevertheless some differences; namely, for the Orthodox Church, state and church are still intrinsically interwoven. It took the Catholic Church centuries to free itself from the state. The Catholics refer to the Holy Spirit "from the Father and the Son" the Orthodox "from the Father through the Son." The formulas are equivalent; therefore it makes no difference. Another difference concerns the councils. Both sides agree that ecumenical councils have the ability to infallibly define doctrine, but a question arises concerning which councils are ecumenical. The Eastern Orthodox communion bases its teaching on Scripture and the seven ecumenical councils–First Council of Nicaea (325), First Council of Constantinople (381), Council of Ephesus (431), Council of Chalcedon (451), Second Council of Constantinople (553), Third Council of Constantinople (680), and Second Council of Nicaea (787). Catholics recognize these as the first seven ecumenical councils, but not the only seven. While the Catholics recognize an ensuing series of ecumenical councils, leading to Vatican II, which closed in 1965, the Eastern Orthodox say there have been no ecumenical councils since 787, and no teaching after the Second Council of Nicaea is accepted as having universal authority.

Since the Eastern schism began, the Orthodox Church has generally proclaimed that the pope has only a primacy of honor among the bishops of the world, not a primacy of authority, which resulted in the Eastern fragmentation. Islam gave military protection to the center of the Eastern Orthodox world, but at a high price. The Muslim sultan sold the office of patriarch to the highest bidder and changed the occupants often, to rake in more money. From 1443 to 1923, the Turkish sultans deposed 105 out of 159 patriarchs. Six were murdered, and only 21 died of natural causes while in office.

The patriarch's authority was further weakened by Ivan the Great who called himself Czar meaning Caesar. Moscow was called the third Rome, and the Czar tried to assume the role to protect Eastern Christianity. The Eastern Church lost its center, and fragmentation along national lines ensued. Russia claimed independence from the patriarchate of Constantinople in 1589, the first nation to do so. Other ethnic and regional splintering quickly followed, and today there are eleven independent Orthodox Churches. The Russian Orthodox Church dominates contemporary Eastern Orthodoxy with seven-eights of the total number of Orthodox

Christians. The Byzantine Greeks in Italy and the Maronites of Syria retained communion with Rome.

Reconciliation attempts failed in the past, but what separates the Catholics from the Orthodox is little compared to what unites them. Over the last several decades, there has been a marked lessening of tensions and an overcoming of long-standing hostilities.

In 1965, Pope Paul VI and Patriarch Athenagoras I of Constantinople lifted mutual excommunications dating back from the eleventh century, and in 1995, Pope John Paul II and Patriarch Bartholomew II of Constantinople concelebrated the Eucharist together. Pope John Paul II has been tireless in promoting unity between Catholics and Orthodox, Christians already united in their faith in Jesus Christ.

Protestantism

Protestant is the name applied to any follower of a religious group that separated from the Catholic Church at the time of the Protestant Reformation. It includes all followers of the many offshoots of the original bodies. The term was first used when Frederick of Saxony and others protested against the Diet's degree permitting Catholic worship (Diet of Speyer in 1529). Martin Luther (1483–1546) is regarded as the father of the Protestant Reformation, but there were forerunners with strikingly similar beliefs. The two most notable were Wycliffe and Hus.

John Wycliffe

John Wycliffe (1320–1384) the English reformer denounced the worldliness of the popes and emphasized the spiritual freedom of the righteous man. The denial of transubstantiation gave his enemies the last straw. He was denied access to Oxford University and his followers were expelled. He was condemned as a heretic. He died at his parish at Lutterworth of natural causes. The mediating priesthood and the sacrificial masses of the medieval church were no longer essential. Thus Wycliffe anticipates Luther's doctrine of justification by faith alone.

John Hus

John Hus (1369–1415), the Czech reformer and avid disciple of Wycliffe, viewed Christ, not the pope, as the head of the church. When he openly attacked the pope's sale of indulgences, Prague fell under a papal interdict because of Hus. So Hus lost his support of King Wencelas. The reformer left for exile to Southern Bohemia. During his exile, Hus intensely studied Wycliffe's writings and produced his major work *On the Church*. Hus was also condemned as a heretic; he went to the Council of Basle under a safe-conduct from Emperor Sigismund to plead his cause. At Basle, however, he was put on trial and burned at the stake.

Martin Luther

Luther, an Augustinian, Catholic monk, was a most controversial figure, to say the least. Depending on who is talking– he is a Protestant hero, a freedom fighter, a wise and insightful church leader or a heretic, an apostate, a profane ecclesiastical terrorist, a necessary evil. Who was he in reality? I leave that up to the reader.

It all began in 1507, when Pope Julius II granted a plenary indulgence to help to pay for the rebuilding of Saint Peter's. His successor renewed that grant. The plenary indulgence had not been preached in Wittenberg, the part of Germany where Martin Luther was stationed as a young university professor. The elector of Saxony had a remarkable collection of relics in his castle at Wittenberg. In 1516, Pope Leo had granted an indulgence to anyone who visited the elector's display for a small fee. The elector wanted no competition, but the Archbishop Albrecht of Mainz prevailed upon the pope to allow the preaching of the plenary indulgence in his diocese. He needed money, and half of the proceeds would go to him. A Dominican preacher was appointed in January 1517 to do just that.

Johann Tetzel

Johann Tetzel zealously preached and sold indulgences throughout Germany as well as on the borders of Saxony. Among his customers were Luther's parishioners. Luther noticed fewer people going to confession. That troubled Luther greatly. The theology concerning indulgences was greatly misunderstood by the clergy and faithful alike. At first, Luther objected to the trafficking of indulgences, but when the archbishop failed to reply to his concerns, Luther published his ninety five theses, which marked the start of the Protestant Reformation on October 31, 1517.

Indulgences

How could a little thing like indulgences create a revolution: the Protestant Reformation? The problem lies in a misconception of what indulgences are. Even today there is ignorance on both sides: the Catholics and the non-Catholics. Michael Walsh, a former Jesuit for twenty years, gives this definition: "The basic understanding is that an indulgence is a remission of the penance imposed by the Church for some serious sin which has been confessed and forgiven" (Walsh, 1984, p. 143). This definition is flawed because his statement, "a remission of the penance imposed by the Church" is incorrect. It is rather a negation of temporal punishment, not imposed by the church but as a consequence of sin that is either partially or totally removed.

Here is the Catholic Church's definition: "An indulgence is a remission before God of the temporal punishment due to sins whose guilt has already been forgiven, which the faithful Christian who is duly disposed gains under certain defined conditions" (Catholic Catechism, 1997, article 1471).

The Protestants accused the Catholics of buying their salvation with money, but indulgences have nothing to do with salvation as such. Nowadays a common practice among Protestants is to, "Sow a seed [money in most cases] for the salvation of a loved one." The very thing they accused the Catholics of hundreds of years ago, they do themselves. Is it wrong? Of course not. The seed, the money, which is matter, is used to produce a spiritual favor. Sowing and reaping is a principle in God's kingdom, a way of working our redemption.

There had been abuses in granting indulgences, so in 1567 Pope Pius V canceled all grants of indulgences involving any fees or other financial transactions. In fact, there was never an outright selling of indulgences but the giving of alms (money) to works of charity, giving to the poor and widows. The person's inward attitude and his personal loving relationship with God were the determining factors in gaining an indulgence. Love covers all sins and the punishments connected with sin. Pope Paul VI stated, "Indulgences cannot be gained without a sincere conversion of outlook and unity with God." Indulgences are sacramentals, just one of God's many ways to impart temporal or eternal favors to His children. There are indulgences connected with the reading of Scriptures. Both Protestants and Catholics who do not believe in indulgences still reap the benefits. One signing the cross while saying, "In the name of the Father, and of the Son, and of the Holy Spirit. Amen," is also granted an indulgence. Protestants often mock Catholics for it. It is the most frequently used sacramental of the Catholic Church. It is a symbol of our salvation, the cross on which Christ died. Done with faith, it applies the benefits of the cross to one's life by calling upon God the Father, God the Son and God the Holy Spirit. The closest equivalent to the sign of the cross for the Protestants is "applying the blood of Jesus" by faith to one's life. The signing of the cross is much more than "applying the blood of Jesus" to one's life; it is the total redemptive endeavor of the Godhead applied to one's life.

Coming back to Luther

Albrecht complained to Rome. But there was little to upset the pope in Luther's theses. Nevertheless they revealed strong doubts about papal primacy. In *On the Papacy at Rome,* published by Luther, he argued that the pope was only a symbolic figure of unity and that the true church was invisible, being the community of all believers. In 1522, Luther abolished the office of the bishop including the office of the pope. Luther believed that the pope was the anti-Christ. In 1545, the Council of Trent began without the presence of Protestant representation, but they were present at a later date. They demanded that everything discussed before their arrival be gone through again; further they required the abolition of bishops' oaths of loyalty to the papacy; they also refused to deal directly with papal legates. This was the worst mistake Luther and his followers could have possibly made. What Luther did was a rebellion against authority, the abolition of God's divine order by getting rid of Apostles (bishops). According to him, he found no warrant for them in Scriptures. Was he not only rebellious but blind too? Most Protestant denominations have no bishops—no apostles and no common leadership, no central command. Just imagine an army without a central command; chaos would be the result. It shows among Protestant denominations. They proliferate enormously, with more than four hundred offshoots in the U.S.A. alone. Each believes in the Scriptures but interprets its content differently.

> And in the church God has appointed first of all apostles, second prophets, third teachers, then workers of miracles, also those of having gifts of healing, those able to help others, those with gifts of administration, and those speaking in different kinds of tongues" (1 Corinthians 12:28 NIV).

Even Jesus Himself submitted to the established order of the apostles, the man of God, the priest. That is the only way of salvation. Jesus, the Son of God, would not bypass the man of God in authority.

> Then Jesus came from Galilee to the Jordan to be baptized by
> John. But John tried to deter him, saying, "I need to be baptized by
> you, and do you come to me?"
>
> Jesus replied, "Let it be so now; it is proper for us to do this to
> fulfill all righteousness" (Matthew 3:13–15 NIV).

So many are deceived. If four hundred denominations believe something differently, obviously at best only one can be truthful and all others teach and believe a lie. Such a thing will not happen in the Catholic Church with the pope as their leader in conjunction with all apostles (bishops) guided above all by the Holy Spirit. Catholics are assured of truthfulness in their doctrine, a doctrine that does not have to be reinvented over and over again.

The priesthood also fell under Luther's axe. With his conviction that salvation comes by faith in Christ Jesus alone, priests became superfluous. The man of God was no longer needed. The celebration of the Eucharist, the administration of the sacraments, the mediation of the priests all crumbled into insignificance. Luther retained only two sacraments: baptism and the Lord's Supper. He even placed these two within a community of believing Christians, rather than in the hands of the priesthood. The whole emphasis in worship changed from the celebration of the mass to the preaching and teaching of God's Word. "...to be a minister of Christ Jesus to the Gentiles with the priestly duty of proclaiming the gospel of God, so that the Gentiles might become an offering acceptable to God, sanctified by the Holy Spirit" (Romans 15:16 NIV). The priest is the spiritual father of his flock. Under him the children of God mature to become sons and daughters of God. No father—no sons or daughters. Only sons and daughters are part of the priesthood, children have no authority, nor do they operate in the gifts of the Holy Spirit. Children are tossed to and fro. One noticeable phenomenon seen among Protestants is the hopping from church to church. Spiritually undernourished children are the result. Infighting is another trait of Protestant churches, they often split and divide. Remember, only sons of God are led by the Holy Spirit.

Luther proclaimed two key doctrinal statements, both in stark contrast to the Catholic Churches' views and beliefs. He made a great fuss about "justification by faith alone and not by good works." Some people change the word justification to salvation. Even the word salvation is given different meanings. Being born of God, born from above or born again is not salvation but its first step. Being born of God is a free gift from God and to be truly saved requires a lifetime of cooperation with God.

"For we are God's workmanship, created in Christ Jesus to do good works, which God prepared in advance for us to do" (Ephesians 2:10 NIV).

The Council of Trent (Sess. 3, ch. 8 and 3) declared the following.

> Faith is the beginning of man's salvation (being born of God), the foundation and root of all justification; without which (that is faith) it is impossible to please God and to obtain fellowship with his Son.
>
> Faith is man's assent to revealed truth. It is thus the base of justification. We are justified by faith and good works as James 2:24 & 26 declares, "You see that a person is justified by what he does and not by faith alone. As the body without the spirit is dead so faith without deeds is dead" (NIV). It must be stressed however that a man is not justified by observing the law, but by faith in Jesus Christ.

Interestingly, for many Protestants, the view of a canonized saint of the Catholic Church is this: A saint is one who has performed a super abundance of good works and is, therefore, above all others to be praised. This definition could apply to anyone. The real definition of a saint is as follows: A saint is a true believer, Christ in him and he in Christ, fully matured, a son of God in whom the fruits of the Holy Spirit are manifested and the gifts of the Spirit are in operation. A very small number of saints are officially recognized by the Catholic Church. Most of them, if not all of them, still operate in the gifts of the Holy Spirit even though they have passed on to eternal life. So miracles still occur through their intercession.

Luther's second doctrinal statement has to do with the Eucharist. His theory called consubstantiation, existence of God's presence in the Eucharist, was that the body and blood of Jesus Christ coexisted with the substances of bread and wine. Again, it is in strong contrast to the Catholic view of transubstantiation, that the sacramental bread and wine changed into the body and blood of Jesus Christ when consecrated during the mass. Many Protestants, while taking communion declare that they take the symbols of His body and blood, bread and wine. Jesus' words in Matthew 26:26–28 clear the controversy:

> While they were eating, Jesus took bread, gave thanks and broke it,
> and gave it to his disciples, saying, "Take and eat; this is my body."
> Then he took the cup, gave thanks and offered it to them, saying,
> "Drink from it, all of you. This is my blood of the covenant, which is
> poured out for many for the forgiveness of sins (NIV).

Jesus did not say, "This is the symbol of my body nor the symbol of my blood but this is my body, this is my blood." It is the spiritual, which is unseen, manifested in the natural, matter, which is seen.

The Gospel of John, chapter six, provides further insight into this issue:

> "I am the living bread that came down from heaven. If anyone eats of this bread, he will live forever. This bread is my flesh, which I will give for the life of the world."
>
> Then the Jews began to argue sharply among themselves, "How can this man give us his flesh to eat?"
>
> Jesus said to them, "I tell you the truth, unless you eat the flesh of the Son of Man and drink his blood, you have no life in you. Whoever eats my flesh and drinks my blood has eternal life, and I will raise him up at the last day. For my flesh is real food and my blood is real drink. Whoever eats my flesh and drinks my blood remains in me, and I in him (John 6:51-56 NIV).
>
> On hearing it, many of his disciples said, "This is a hard teaching. Who can accept it? (John 6:60 NIV).
>
> From this time many of his disciples turned back and no longer followed him (John 6:66 NIV).

It couldn't be more explicit. When the bread and wine is consecrated, a transubstantiation takes place; the bread and wine look the same, but in reality they are the flesh and blood of Jesus Christ.

Luther, who rebelled against the established authority of popes and bishops, also lashed out against the peasants who rebelled against the German princes. At first, he recognized the justice of the peasants' complaints. In his pamphlet, *Against the Thievish and Murderous Hordes of Peasant*, Luther asked the princes to "knock down, strangle and stab … and think nothing so venomous, pernicious, or Satanic as an insurgent" (Against the Thievish and Murderous Hordes of Peasant, as cited in Shelby, 1995, p. 243). More than one hundred thousand were killed. The surviving peasants considered Luther a false prophet, and many returned to the Roman Catholic Church or turned to more radical forms of reformation. Luther's views allowed the princes to control the churches in their territories, strengthening their power and wealth.

Luther denounced reformers who disagreed with him, and there were a lot of disagreements. In his attacks, he used terms that he once reserved for the papacy. His statements about the Jews would have made a Hitler blush. On the positive side, Luther translated the New Testament into German while imprisoned in the castle of Wartburg in just ten weeks. He also implemented a celebration of the Mass for Germans in their own language instead of Latin, hundreds of years ahead of Vatican II, which implemented the Mass in the vernacular of the local community throughout the world.

The Protestants

Protestantism excludes traditional Christianity based upon church authority. Protestant Christianity adheres broadly to three predominant principles:

1. The supremacy of the Scriptures as the sole source and means of doctrine, excluding Apostolic tradition.

2. The reasoning that justification is by faith alone.

3. The role of priesthood belongs to all believers.

Among the various denominations, there are vast differences of interpretation of these principles with equally great innovations of dogmatic understanding.

There are four major original Protestant denominations: Lutherans, Anabaptists, Reformed and Anglicans. Out of these four, many others proceeded. The divisions and re-divisions are still going on to this very day.

The Lutherans

Even with recognizing historical differences, the Lutherans are still closer to Catholics then they are to others Protestant groups. For the last 40 years, attempts have been and are still being made to reconcile Lutherans and Catholics. Several statements and discussions have been made by joint sessions of the Roman Catholic and Lutheran ecumenical bodies with the most recent being on Saints in glory, Mary and the Saints, and several of the holy people for biblical data.

The Lutheran belief arose from the teachings made up and taught by Martin Luther (1546) in Erfurt and Wittenburg, Germany. It finds its center in a justification by faith alone, based on Luther's translation of Romans 3:28. Luther held that original justice was con-natural to Adam and Eve, and original sin so corrupted human nature that man could no longer do good, for this reason he had degenerated, and his free will had been taken from him. Christ's redemption was entirely done for us. There is no need for further effort on man's part, either in imitation of Christ or personal merit. It follows that habitual grace is nonexistent; actual grace is God working in us. One needs only to have faith. Luther did away with sacraments, keeping only baptism and a non-consecrated Eucharist where Christ is only present by the faith of the believer. There is no need for an established priesthood, since truth comes from the Bible, which is freely interpreted. Luther also denied purgatory, indulgences, prayers for the dead and the intercession of the saints. To learn more about purgatory, prayers for the departed, intercession of the saints and saint worship refer to Appendix B.

The Anabaptists

Anabaptism had its beginning in the village Zollikon near Zurich in January 1525. Its doctrine was derived from key Lutheran beliefs, but neither Luther, Calvin, nor Zwingli considered the Anabaptists' position favorable. Nevertheless, Anabaptism was another important expression of the Protestant Reformation.

Their main tenet is that baptism is for adults only, and that infant baptism is invalid. They also reject the teaching of the sacraments and the nature of the Catholic Church, and they hold a belief that believers are directly and only influenced by the Holy Spirit. The Anabaptists proved to be the forerunners of most modern Protestants who believe in the separation of church and state.

The Anabaptists lacked cohesiveness. No single body of doctrine and no unifying organization prevailed among them. Even the name Anabaptist was pinned on them by their enemies. Their refusal to abide by a degree of the Zurich Council in regards to infant baptism initiated persecution and death. Many fled to Germany and Austria, but their prospects were not any better there. The imperial Diet of Speyer (1529) proclaimed Anabaptism a heresy and every court in Christendom was obligated to condemn the heretics to death. Many thousands were executed by fire, water and the sword. But all they wanted was a persons' right to his or her own beliefs.

The persecution forced many Anabaptists north where they found refuge on the lands of a tolerant prince in Moravia. They formed communities, which were consolidated under the leadership of Jakob Hutter. These groups were known as the Hutterites.

Many of the twentieth century descendants of the Anabaptists are called Mennonites. Taking the name from Menno Simons (1496–1561) a former Catholic priest who traveled widely to visit and minister to the scattered Anabaptist groups of Northern Europe after the defeat of the Munster rebellion in mid 1530. One branch from the Mennonites, the Old Amish, holds tenaciously to the old ways, while the majority of the Mennonites live a modern life. Distant relatives of the first Anabaptists include the modern day Baptists and Quakers.

The Baptists

Central to the teaching of the Baptists is their doctrine on baptism, which is called an ordinance rather than a sacrament. Baptism is given to adults only and that by immersion. For them, baptism is the sole criteria for salvation but requires that the baptized person accept and pursue a life of virtue. They regard Scriptures as the sole rule of faith, personal justification through faith in Christ. Worship services vary from church to church, including the Lord's Supper which is celebrated at various times and called an ordinance. They are one of the largest Protestant denominations in the U.S.A.

There are several factions among Baptists adhering to changed teaching.

Arminianism: a rejection of the Calvinist teachings on grace and predestination.

Fundamentalism: a belief in a strict interpretation of the Scriptures.

Millenarianism: a belief in a literal interpretation of chapter twenty of the Book of Revelation.

Modernism: a swing towards the individual's interpretation of Scriptures.
Predestinationists: a belief that men's salvation is determined by God's will alone and cannot be changed by virtue or grace.

The Quakers

Quakers is the common or popular name of the members of a small group who are known as the Society of Friends. They were founded in 1648 by George Fox (1624–1691). It was Fox's intention to return to a primitive Christianity. They were not well received and suffered persecution because they were disruptive to other churches' services. The Quakers place great emphasis on education based on religious training. They are opposed to swearing in courts of law.

A famous Quaker in America was William Penn (1644–1718). He obtained a large sum of money from King Charles II of England in payment owed to Penn's father, Sir William Penn of the Admiralty. He then bought a large piece of land in the New World, which we now call Pennsylvania or Penn's wood.

The Reformed Churches

The Reformed churches are a Calvinistic Christianity. John Calvin, French Reformer (1509–1564), has had the greatest influence, other than the work of Martin Luther, in the Reformed churches of Protestantism. When Calvin visited Geneva, he was urged by the inflammatory reformer William Farel to stay and to establish the work of God there. At that time, Geneva's Protestantism rested chiefly on political hostility towards the bishop, not doctrinal conviction. Calvin's leadership shaped a third reformation tradition. Today we call it Reformed or Calvinistic Christianity. It includes all Presbyterians, Dutch and German Reformed Churches, and many Baptists and Congregationalists.

Calvin was a scholar and lawyer, thin in stature, demanding much of himself and of others. Calvin's organizing and executive abilities enabled him to build on the work of Zwingli, whose reform's movement started in Zurich. It spread rapidly in German-speaking Switzerland. In 1531, Zwingli lost his life in the battle of Protestant and Catholic Cantons at Kappel. The leadership fell in the hands of Bullinger, but by the 1540s, Geneva emerged as the international center of Reformed Christianity under Calvin's disciplined direction. He assumed a position of leadership in the Protestant cause.

Zwingli had advocated the abolition of the Mass and the sacrament of penance. He would not accept any presence of Christ in the Eucharist, only a symbolic one that led to dissentions amongst Protestant groups and made union between them impossible.

In 1553, the brilliant but erratic Spanish physician, Michael Servetus, sought refuge in Geneva. He was fleeing Catholic persecution for his heresy of denying the doctrine of the Trinity. Calvin supported the silencing of the ill-balanced thinker. Servetus was burned at the stake, and Calvin is primarily remembered as the man who burned Servetus.

Luther's central doctrine was justification by faith; for Calvin it was God's sovereign will. He kept two sacraments: baptism and the Lord's Supper. For Calvin, man is not justified by works, yet no justified man is without works. No one can be a true Christian without aspiring to holiness in life. A rigorous pursuit of moral righteousness is one of the principal features of Calvinism. Luther tended to consider the state supreme, Calvin thought that no man—whether pope or king— had any claim to absolute power.
Calvinistic resistance to the exercise of arbitrary power by monarchs was a key factor in the development of modern constitutional governments. The church is not subject to secular government except in secular matters, but the church has the obligation to guide the secular authorities in spiritual matters.

In France, Calvin's homeland, Calvinism remained a minority. At one point, due to very influential nobility converts, the French Calvinists, also called the Huguenots, threatened to seize leadership of the country. So, on St. Bartholomew's Day in 1572, thousands of them were ruthlessly killed to never again become a serious threat to the Catholics. Calvinism invaded the Netherlands in opposition to the oppressive rule of Catholic Spain. John Knox, a passionate preacher of Calvinism was instrumental in making Scotland the most devoutly Calvinistic country in the world.

Presbyterians

Presbyterianism is the mainstream of churches that originate from the reformed teaching of John Knox. It takes its name from the form of church system under which it is governed. The basic doctrine of the Presbyterian Churches holds to the sovereignty of God; radical human sinfulness, divine redemption and election, the sole authority of Scriptures in matters of faith and practice and the absolute kingship of Christ.

There is one state-church—Scotland—however this is not a mother church but maintains a spiritual independence. In 1875, the Alliance of Reformed Church was founded with their headquarter in Geneva, Switzerland. It unites those churches that hold the Presbyterian system.

Congregationalists

Congregationalists have their origin in the years between 1570 and 1620. Since then, there have been numerous changes and adoptions of those first Bible groups. One of the principal tenets is that of a gathered church rather than a geographical, national or parochial church. Each church is thus distinct and is said to have a direct covenant with Christ as the head of the universal church. Thus each church has autonomy under the guidance of the Holy Spirit. Congregationalists also propose an interdenominational ecumenism and missionary effort.

The seventeenth-century Congregationalists are the real architects of the denominational theory of the church. It proclaims, that the true church cannot be identified with any single ecclesiastical structure. No denominations can claim to represent the whole church of Christ. Each simply constitutes a different form in worship and organization of the larger picture of the church. Nevertheless, the Congregationalists have no intention to embrace all Christian denominations, only those who share a common understanding of the main Christian faith principles.

The United Church of Christ

Many from the Congregational Christian Churches, the Evangelical Churches and the Reformed Churches merged on June 25, 1957 and became known as the United Church of Christ. Negotiations had started in 1940. The United Church of Christ is governed by a system of
associations and conferences held under a general synod, but each has its own organization and autonomy. They celebrate communion on a regular basis, but Christ is considered only spiritually present in the sacrament.

The Anglicans

This is the name of the members of the established Church of England. The Lutheran Reformation began in a monastic cell, the Anabaptist Reformation in a prayer meeting, the Calvinistic Reformation at a scholar's desk and the English Reformation began in the affairs of state, specifically with the problem of who would succeed to the royal throne.

Henry VIII's marriage problems were a scandal and against the laws of the Catholic Church. He had no son born of his queen, Catherine of Aragon. Henry revolted against the pope and rejected his authority in view of marrying Anne Boleyn. Under Henry, nothing changed doctrinally. Pope Clement VII refused to annul Henry's marriage of eighteen years to Catherine. In January 1533, the king secretly married Anne, and in May an English court declared Henry's marriage to Catherine null and void.

A year later, in 1534, the Act of Supremacy declared, "The King's majesty justly and rightly is and ought to be and shall be reputed the only supreme head in earth of the Church of England called Anglicana Ecclesia" (Shelby, 1995, p. 243). This made the break with Rome complete. England had a national church with the king as its head. He could appoint, but he could not consecrate bishops. He could defend, but he could not formulate the faith.

Only two serious changes marked the new Church of England. First the Catholic Church was persecuted and its properties, especially the monasteries, were seized. Henry used it to replenish the royal coffers, almost one third of the national wealth. The second was the publication of the English Bible for use in the churches.

The publications of a series of articles under King Edward in 1549 and under Queen Elizabeth in 1563 were essentially Protestant. They were worded in such a way to satisfy both the moderates (Episcopalians) and the extremists (Calvinists). Elizabeth brought forth her Acts of Supremacy and Uniformity, which led to legalized persecution of Catholics for nearly 200 years. Those upholding papal authority were accused of committing treason. Pope Pius V excommunicated Queen Elizabeth in 1570.

Since Vatican II, efforts have been made to reconcile the Anglicans and the Catholics.

The Episcopalians

The Episcopalian Church arose from the Anglican Church. In 1789, it adopted a separate name, laws, constitution and a revised version of the Book of Prayers. Protestant Episcopal meant, non-Catholic, but with bishops in authority. The church has three orders: bishops, priests and deacons. The pastor is called rector and is chosen by the vestry, which is an elected group of laity from the parish. Church members consider themselves as belonging to one of three groups: Protestant, a third branch of the Catholic Church (the other two being Roman Catholic and Eastern Orthodox) or a mixture of Protestant and Catholic.

Some very startling events are taking place within the Anglican and the Episcopalian Churches. Anglican bishops recognize gay marriages and so do Episcopalians. In the U.S.A., in late 2003, the Episcopalians ordained a gay bishop. Clearly, this violates Christian doctrine and beliefs. Some of their own churches were closed for refusing to accept such doctrine and a split amongst them is brewing. They no longer constitute a Christian adherence and have fallen into sectarianism. They cut themselves off from the body of Christ and no longer is Christ in them nor they in Christ. They have tarnished their image and likeness of God and no longer should be called Christians because they no longer are. Refer to Appendix C for more information about homosexuality.

The Methodists

The Methodists boast over two hundred million members worldwide. The people called Methodists were a church within a church (1748). The break from the established Anglican Church came in 1684. It was founded by John Wesley (1703–1791). He was a tireless preacher who traveled widely mostly on horseback. He claimed a minimum of 4,500 miles per year average of travel. The name was given to them as a joke because of the exactitude of their liturgical approach to worship. The brother of John Wesley, Charles Wesley (1707–1788) was also active as a founding preacher and so was George Whitefield (1714–1770). Charles wrote over 7,000 hymns. "Jesus lover of my soul" is one of the favorites. In Canada, in 1925, the Methodist Church joined the Congregationalists, and some of the Presbyterians to form the United Church of Canada.

The Pentecostals

The Pentecostals have become the largest family of Protestants in the world today with over two hundred million members worldwide. They have over 11,000 Pentecostal denominations.

The Pentecostal movement first began in England in the eighteenth century and developed in the early twentieth century. Between the years 1925 and 1935, the Jeffrey brothers and their nephew gave the movement a great boost. In America, it was the foundation of the Assemblies of God in 1914 that had a significant influence on the movement. They are now the largest Pentecostal denomination worldwide.

The Pentecostal beliefs are based fundamentally upon the teachings of John Wesley. Other non-Methodist pioneers were Baptist, Quaker and Presbyterian. Their belief is in a second blessing, with Pentecost being the first blessing. It is the sanctification by the Holy Spirit, which one feels, exalted by the direct action of the Holy Spirit. The gifts of the Holy Spirit are supposed to be operational in all Pentecostal Churches and for that matter in all Christian Churches regardless of their denomination.

All true Christian Churches are Pentecostal in nature, referring to the beginning at Pentecost and the nature of operation. It is nothing neither new nor extraordinary. What is extraordinary is that which is basic to Christianity is often forgotten, not well received or not received at all. The Holy Spirit and His redemptive work among humanity were basic at the start of Christianity, still are and ever will be.

As always, when God does something, Satan is quick to counterfeit it, therefore we must judge what is truly of the Holy Spirit and what is not. The manifestations of the Holy Spirit must portray a fidelity to authentic doctrine and the presence of love.

The Independent Non-Denominational Churches

The Independent Churches are not a brand new phenomenon, but they had their origin in the early Congregational Churches, founded during the years from 1570 to 1620. They are Protestant in origin. One of their principal tenets is that of a gathered church, rather than a geographical, local or parochial church. Each church is thus distinct and is said to have a direct covenant with Christ as the head of the Universal Church. Thus each church has autonomy under the guidance of the Holy Spirit. They draw their membership from all denominations, Catholics as well as Orthodox and Protestants. Often their members congregate hours away from their gathering place. A true Independent Church set in place by the Holy Spirit is Pentecostal in nature, a church where the gifts of the Holy Spirit are in operation, and a place where God's presence is manifested.

A true church is a church where Jesus is present, and where Jesus is present, the Father is present, and there the Holy Spirit is present as well. The Catholic Church defines a true catholic church a church where Jesus is present. I personally am a Catholic since birth. Ninety eight percent of my country of origin is Catholic. But God called me to an Independent Non-Denominational Church. I experienced firsthand the stark contrast between the two. For years, I asked myself the question, "Why would God institute churches outside His church, the Catholic Church?" Could He not do in the Catholic Church what He does in the Independent Churches? When it comes to doctrine, I definitely choose the Catholic Church's doctrine. They have not changed since the beginning. Attacks from all sides only made them define their doctrine more clearly. Their doctrine is totally based on Scriptures, Jesus promised them they would not err because of the Holy Spirit. And that is still valid today almost 2000 years later.

To find the answer, I looked at the way the Catholic Church conducts a regular service versus the way the Independent Churches conduct their service. God so loved the world that He gave His only Son. Here lies the answer. God is not so much interested in how a service is conducted; rather He is interested in the people being saved, born from above, born of Him, delivered, set free, and healed in spirit, mind and body. Interestingly most of the Independent Churches were birthed in the last 20 years. A great harvest of souls is ready worldwide; we are in the last days. The Independent Churches are in the forefront of world evangelism with evangelists originating from all denominations.

Here are a few reasons why God chooses Independent Churches to do His work:

First is the way a person is called into the ministry, be it as an apostle, prophet, evangelist, teacher or pastor. Jesus chose unlearned people, rough people with little or no education like the fishermen. Beside that, He chose learned people like the tax collector and the doctor and some highly educated in doctrine like Paul the Apostle. In the Catholic Church there is only one way to access the ministry, and that is through the seminary and university schooling. A murderer, a junkie, a drug addict and an illiterate, therefore, have no chance whatsoever. Alternately, God can call and choose whomever He likes, whomever He wants to choose. I know personally of a native Indian who lived as a drunkard for 27 years in a cardboard box on skid road in Vancouver. Yet God called that man to be a minister to the native people in British Colombia. It all came to pass through an Independent Church in Vancouver.

The second reason is that in the Catholic Church no women are ordained even though there were women apostles in Bible times. Women can minister God's love to His people in a way no man can. Today there are numerous tremendously gifted and anointed women pastors, prophets, apostles, evangelists and teachers in the Independent Churches, all called and chosen by God Almighty. Who is to say women cannot be ministers? Yes, women are educators in Catholic schools and in the mission field as doctors, nurses etc. or in the ministry of helps but not in the five-fold ministry.

Thirdly, possibly the most important reason of all has to do with the Holy Spirit. The Holy Spirit needs total freedom of operation to do His redemptive work among the people. A few, very few even among the Independent Churches provide that freedom for the Holy Spirit. Most churches are busy doing what is required, following a certain procedure, conducting the services according to tradition leaving little or no room for the Holy Spirit. The ministers and priests must be in tune with the Holy Spirit, hear Him and obey Him. If not, the Holy Spirit does not force the issue. He will be grieved and leave. In many churches the services are rigidly performed, and the Holy Spirit is boxed in. Nothing will happen to set the captives free, to deliver the oppressed and to heal the sick. God never overrides the established authority. He always works through His ministers and priests, and if they do not allow Him to move freely, He has no choice than to leave and go elsewhere.

Fourthly, denominationalism places a limitation on the kind of attendance you may expect. Catholics go to a Catholic church, Baptists to a Baptist church and so forth. But for Independent Churches, there is no denominational label, and anyone is welcome no matter what their denomination is or the lack of it. The Holy Spirit has it easy to draw unbelievers, Buddhists, Hindus, etc., murderers, and drug addicts to such churches and set them free.

The Christian family is broad and manifold. They represent the body of Christ. It is His fullness manifested on earth. Criticism is definitely out of place. One must look behind the apparent differences and strive for a perfect faith (belief system) in love and obedience under the guidance of the Holy Spirit.

8. How Do I Become A Christian?

To become a Christian one must be born from above, born of God. But it does not stop there, that is just the beginning, the start. The new birth must be developed, and it takes one's doing to do that; it takes a lifetime. The new birth is a free gift from God, given by grace. You do not work for it. To become a Christian is often referred to as salvation.

Non-Christians are often asked, "Are you saved?" Their reply is, "From what?" Obviously that is not the proper approach nor is it correct. Being born of God and being saved are two different aspects of being a Christian. One is born of God by grace but saved by good works.

Christianity was never meant to be difficult; in fact, it is so simple. Becoming a Christian is basic Christian doctrine, but, even here, Satan tries everything to deceive humanity. In John 3:3 and 7, Jesus told Nicodemus, "I tell you the truth, no one can see the kingdom of God unless he is born again." "You should not be surprised at my saying, 'You must be born again!'" (NIV). "In all truth I tell you, no one can see the kingdom of God without being born from above!" "Do not be surprised when I say: you must be born from above" (John 3: 3 and 7, NJB). Here we have the same Bible verses from different translations. In most of the translations we find "born again" but in the NJB translation "born from above". The original Greek text says: *gennatha anothen*. *Gennatha* means born and *anothen* can be translated either again or from above. It occurs only twice in the Bible where some of the translators used the word 'again' others used the words 'from above'. For a non-believer the expression 'born from above' is more easily understood than 'born again'. Unless one has a clear understanding what the expression 'born again' stands for, one is better off to use the expression 'born from above'.

At your physical birth, born of your earthly parents, you were born a stillbirth—spirit, mind and body—dead in God's eyes. God's life was not in you, neither in your spiritual nature nor in your physical nature. Satan had a hold on you, spirit, mind and body. You were lost forever. If one could see in the spiritual realm, what a difference would be noticeable between a Christian and a non-Christian. Within the Christian family, the Catholics prefer 'born from above', while the Protestants prefer 'born again'.

We live in a material world and to interact in that world humans need to have a natural, physical body. The body is created from the dust of the earth and will return to the dust of the earth. At the moment your spirit separates from your body you die physically. "As the body without the spirit is dead, so faith without deeds is dead" (James 2:26 NIV). At the time of physical death, unless you are born of God, you are totally dead—spirit, mind and body. Although your spirit is dead, it does not cease to exist. For the born of God believer, the mind and body will be resurrected at the Rapture.

Your body is the seed for your eternal body in heaven. It is sown a natural body and raised a spiritual body, a glorified body.

> So will it be with the resurrection of the dead. The body that is sown
> is perishable, it is raised imperishable; it is sown in dishonor, it is
> raised in glory; it is sown in weakness, it is raised in power; it is
> sown a natural body, it is raised a spiritual body (1 Corinthians
> 15:42–44 NIV).

The born of God believer becomes God's dwelling place. "If anyone destroys God's temple, God will destroy him; for God's temple is sacred, and you are that temple" (1 Corinthians 3:17 NIV). Anyone who is not born of God is greatly hampered in all that he does.

How Do I Become Born of God?

A person had no say when he or she was birthed by their parents, but everybody has a say whether he or she will be born spiritually, born from above, born of God, born a second time, born again.

> In all truth I tell you, no one can enter the kingdom of God without
> being born through water and the Spirit; what is born of human
> nature is human; [first time around] what is born of the Spirit is
> spirit [second birth, born again] (John 3:5 NJB).

"Whoever believes and is baptized will be saved; whoever does not believe will be condemned" (Mark 16:16 NJB). To be born of God, one must believe, believe in Jesus Christ and in all that He stands for. Second century candidates for Christianity professed the Old Roman Creed as a baptismal confession:

> I believe in God Almighty
> And in Christ Jesus, his only Son, our Lord

Who was born of the Holy Spirit and the Virgin Mary
Who was crucified under Pontius Pilate and was buried
And the third day rose from the dead
Who ascended into heaven
And sits on the right hand of the Father
Whence he comes to judge the living and the dead.
And in the Holy Ghost
The holy church
The remission of sins
The resurrection of the flesh
The life everlasting (As cited in Stravinskas, 1987).

Nowadays the Nicene Creed (A.D. 325) is used as profession of faith.

We believe in one God the Father, the Almighty, maker of heaven
and earth, of all that is seen and unseen.
We believe in one Lord, Jesus Christ, the only Son of God,
Eternally begotten of the Father, God from God, Light from Light,
true God from true God, begotten not made, one in being with the
Father. Through him all things were made. For us men and for our
salvation he came down from heaven: by the power of the Holy
Spirit he was born of the Virgin Mary, and became man.
For our sake he was crucified under Pontius Pilate; he suffered, died
and was buried. On the third day he rose again in fulfillment of the
Scriptures; he ascended into heaven and is seated at the right hand
of the Father.
He will come again in glory to judge the living and the dead.
And his kingdom will have no end.
We believe in the Holy Spirit, the Lord, the giver of life,
Who proceeds from the Father and the Son.
With the Father and the Son he is worshiped and glorified.
He has spoken through the prophets.
We believe in one holy catholic and apostolic Church.
We acknowledge one baptism for the forgiveness of sins.
We look for the resurrection of the dead, and the life of the world to
come. Amen (As cited in Broderick, 1987, p. 142).

The restoration, the salvation, that new life of Jesus is free. You do not have to earn it, but you must ask for it; it does not come to you automatically. God respects your free will, even if it means that you may be lost forever. Four action words describe the course you must take to become born of God, to become a child of God:

Ask

You must ask Jesus to come into your heart. (Not your physical heart but the heart of your spirit) You invite Him into your dwelling.

Change Course

You ask for forgiveness for all that is wrong in your life, to save you and to set you free. And you determine to change course, to change position, to turn away from a sin position. Sin is a willful transgression of a natural or spiritual law. Those laws never change.

Believe

You believe in your heart that Jesus Christ is the Son of the Living God. You accept Him and He will accept you. Faith is the operating mode of your spirit.

Confess

You confess with your mouth that Jesus Christ is your Lord, Redeemer and Savior. Words, spoken words are powerful. The whole universe, including humankind, was created by spoken words not thoughts.

Here is a simple declaration that can bring you from darkness to light, from death to life, from bondage to freedom. It is the most important and the most powerful thing you can ever do for yourself; no one else can do it for you. Catholics call it life-giving prayer and the Protestants call it the sinner's prayer.

> Jesus, come into my heart and I will live for you. I ask you to forgive me, to save me and to set me free. I believe in my heart that you are the Son of the Living God and I declare that you are my Savior and Lord.

You may ask yourself, "What changed the moment I received and accepted Jesus Christ?" The characteristics of the restored spirit, mind and body give you the answer.

Characteristics of the Restored Spirit, Mind and Body

1. The image and likeness of God is restored.

2. The spirit is still made out of the very essence of God.

3. The spirit is again alive, born of God. Sickness and disease, which may befall the mind and body, can be overcome with spiritual power given to the believer. Again, men and women can live in divine health. "...by his wounds you have been healed" (1 Peter 2:24 NIV).

4. The spirit is alive eternally unless one would renounce Jesus Christ. The lifespan is still set at about 120 years, but the mind and body of those who died before the Rapture will be resurrected at the Rapture. They will have a glorified body and mind. Those who live (the believers) while the Rapture occurs will be changed in an instant to a glorified body and mind. The glorified body and mind is immortal and eternal. "For as in Adam all die, so in Christ all will be made alive" (1 Corinthians 15:22 NIV).

5. The will is free to make the right choices. One can decide which influence to follow. The conscience can again give clear guidance. "How much more, then, will the blood of Christ, who through the eternal Spirit offered himself unblemished to God, cleanse our consciences from acts that lead to death, so that we may serve the living God!" (Hebrews 9:14 NIV).

6. Power and authority is given to the spirit, mind and body in the name of Jesus Christ.

7. The spirit is held captive by the mind and body until physical death occurs or until the Rapture takes place when body and mind will be glorified. The body and mind will be affected by time and space until the Rapture.

8. The spirit, mind and body are again able to operate in perfect faith because the "measure of faith" is given to every born of God person.

9. The believer is able to walk in the spirit, in a loving relationship and fellowship with God.

10. The curse is broken. The believer can choose between blessing and cursing.

The born of God experience is a one-time experience. To live daily in victory, you must use, daily, the power given to you. As the restoration was not automatic, so is the victorious life not automatic. You must use, daily, your will to choose between good and evil, between blessing and cursing. Adam and Eve were created adults—spirit, mind and body. We are born babies—spirit, mind and body. For us there is a process of growing and maturing involved.

To believe and to profess your faith in Jesus Christ is but the first step to become born of God. As Mark 16:16 proclaims, "Whoever believes and is baptized will be saved" (NIV). So, baptism is the other step. Here Catholics and many Protestants differ greatly. For Catholics, you must be baptized; it is a sacrament. For Protestants, it is regarded as an ordinance and regarded as optional. Catholics profess and are baptized at the same time, as for the Protestants, depending on their affiliation, baptism may come anytime, weeks, months, years later or not at all.

Baptism

Baptism is absolutely necessary. Jesus Himself affirmed it in John 3:5, "In all truth I tell you, no one can enter the kingdom of God without being born through water and the Spirit" (NJB) and in John 3:22 we read, "Jesus went with his disciples into the Judean countryside and stayed there with them there and baptized" (NJB).

In Acts, the apostles did the same. "They accepted what he [the apostle Peter] said and were baptized! That very day about three thousand were added to their number" (Acts 2:41 NJB). The Protestant Martin Luther himself was convinced of the necessity of baptism. He wrote:

> Baptism is no human plaything but is instituted by God Himself. Moreover, it is solemnly and strictly commanded and we must be baptized or we shall not be saved. We are not to regard it as an indifferent matter, then, like putting on a new red coat. It is of the greatest importance that we regard baptism as excellent, glorious, and exalted" (Large Catechism 4:6, found in *Triglot Concordia: The Symbolical Books of the Ev. Lutheran Church*).

As a Christian it is hard to believe that many profess Jesus Christ but are not baptized even though the effects of baptism are so tremendous.

The Effects of Baptism

The baptismal effects are manifold. Those outstanding effects of water baptism should convince even the most reluctant person of its necessity.

Forgiveness of Sins

"'You must repent,' Peter answered, 'and every one of you must be baptized in the name of Jesus Christ **for the forgiveness of your sins, and you will receive the gift of the Holy Spirit'**" (Acts 2:38 NJB). All the sins a person ever committed will be forgiven and remembered no more. Once that happens, the baptized person receives the gift of the Holy Spirit. He, the Holy Spirit will dwell in him.

The Holy Spirit

The Holy Spirit is a spirit, the Father is a spirit and the Son is a spirit. We humans are created in the likeness and image of God. We are foremost spirits having a mind and a physical body. Our spirit is our true self. Unless a person is born of God, his or her spirit is dead and he or she does not have God's life in him or her.

For many believers, the Holy Spirit is mostly a mysterious figure, and, for some, He is an 'it' or even a ghost. Some older Bible versions use the word 'ghost' for the Holy Spirit. It conveys the wrong meaning to the people at large. He is not a ghost but a loving, holy God. Holiness characterizes the Holy Spirit. In fact He is the only holy person besides God the Father and God the Son. He is the **Holy** Spirit. Holiness is a unique trait of His character; it denotes truthfulness, perfection and eternal beauty. There are symbols that characterize the Holy Spirit.

Doves live in the wild; they are free whereas pigeons are domesticated and are constrained. Most people do not know that doves give milk. Dove eggs are never incubated and, for that reason, baby doves need the mother to nurse them. When a person accepts Jesus Christ, he or she becomes a new creation by the power of the Holy Spirit. The new believer is an offspring of the Holy Spirit and there is no substitute for the Holy Spirit. For new believers spiritual food is likened to milk. As the dove mother nurses her young, so does the Holy Spirit nurse the new believers if they let Him. Without the Holy Spirit, you cannot grow spiritually.

Wind means spirit, breath and life. The Greek word for spirit literally means wind. Wind, fire and light are either beneficial or destructive. If God's wrath is upon you, you will not escape. You cannot dictate to the wind, it does as it wills. Wind cannot be put into a box, nor can it be contained. Wind is free to move wherever it likes to move. Wind is unpredictable in its operation. Wind is invisible but can be seen by its effects. Wind is indispensable. Stagnant air or water breeds putrefaction and death. A church where the wind of the Holy Spirit does not blow is dead, and the same holds true for you if you are part of that church. Wind is life giving, wind is irresistible. In the winnowing process, wind is used to separate the chaff from the grain. Chaff symbolizes worthlessness, evil or wicked people.

The presence of the Holy Spirit is always characterized by a beneficial warmth and peace, in opposition to the presence of the devil or any demonic presence where coldness and hopelessness make your blood freeze in the veins. Fire gives off heat and warmth; it creates an atmosphere of peace where healing and restoration of spirit, mind and body can take place. Fire can destroy and exterminate the enemy, and fire that fills the believer who is in the hands of the Holy Spirit will destroy the enemy in and around you. Fire purifies to a very high degree. It refines gold, removing all imperfections without destroying the gold. Besides purging, purifying and refining, fire consumes. No one can stand in God's presence unless purified by God's consuming fire. He consumes everything that is not of Him, including you as soon as you come close to Him.

The Holy Spirit is light. Without Him, you are in total darkness. It is the Holy Spirit who enables you to understand the truth, the word of God. It is He who is the guiding light who leads you to Jesus, the light of the world. Without light there is no growth in your spirit, mind or body. By nature we are light dependent and therefore light seekers. Lack of light produces distorted spirits, heresies, and for many, darkness becomes light, wrong becomes right and right becomes wrong. That means people believe as truth what is a lie and believe what is the truth as though it is a lie.

There are times the Holy Spirit acts upon you as a dove, wind, fire or light. For that to happen, you must be in a receptive state, in a state where you actively welcome the Holy Spirit. He respects you so much that He never forces Himself upon you. He is a real gentleman. Your spirit cannot grow nor mature unless the Holy Spirit is involved with you. He gives you life and freedom, transforms, renews, helps, leads, points out, confirms, shows, teaches, instructs, counsels, enlightens, makes to understand, reveals, gives dreams and visions, intercedes, searches, encourages, strengthens, predicts, warns, keeps you from harm, admonishes, compels, convicts, witnesses, testifies, determines, brings to remembrance, controls, distributes, cleanses with water, cleanses with fire, sanctifies and gives rest.

"It is the baptism corresponding to this water which saves you now—not the washing off of physical dirt but **the pledge of a good conscience** given to God through the resurrection of Jesus Christ" (1 Peter 3:21 NJB).

The Conscience
The conscience is an important part of everybody's spirit. It is the faculty that lets you distinguish between good and evil. It is humankind's inborn consciousness of a sense of right and wrong. It is a guiding recognition of right and wrong pertaining to your actions and the motives of your actions. It is your conscience that decides upon the moral standard of your actions and of your motives. It is that inner awareness of conforming to God's will or departing from it, resulting in a sense of approval or condemnation.

When your spirit is not born of God—dead in God's eyes—your conscience is not alive either. Nevertheless, your conscience is such a marvelous faculty created by God that even then you are able to recognize God. Romans 1:20 states, "For since the creation of the world God's invisible qualities—his eternal power and divine nature—have been clearly seen, being understood from what has been made, so that men are without excuse" (NIV) The human conscience bears witness to the existence of God.

A process of growth for maturity is required, which will not end until our spirit joins God in heaven. That growth can either be hastened or hampered depending upon us and the influences we allow to act upon our conscience.

You have enemies: yourself, the world and evil spirits. The world in this context means untruthfulness originating from persons other than you or from yourself. Evil spirits are Satan, demons and fallen angels.

You have friends: yourself, other persons, the Holy Spirit and good spirits (angels). Friends in this context means truthfulness originating from persons other than you, from yourself or from good spirits.

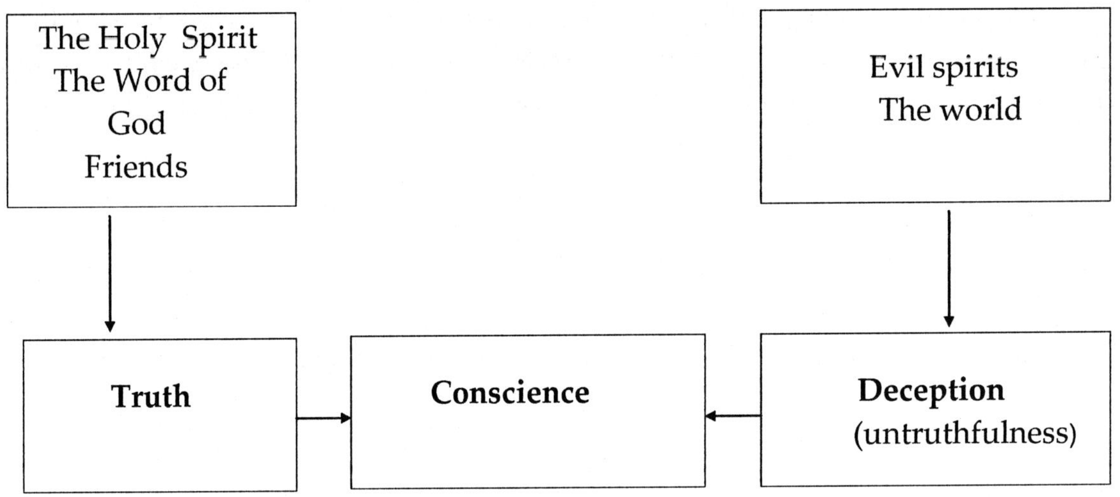

You yourself may influence your conscience in a good way or in a bad way. We train our conscience by the constant use of the Word of God. "But solid food is for the mature, who by constant use have trained themselves to distinguish good from evil" (Hebrews 5:14 NIV). Under wrong influences the conscience becomes defiled, polluted and evil. Such a conscience has been seared as with a hot iron, deceived to a high degree, unable to separate right from wrong.

By the new birth, being born of God, your conscience becomes alive. You yourself were unable to clear your conscience, but now the blood of Jesus Christ will accomplish exactly that, cleansing your conscience from acts that lead to death. The result is a pure, good and perfect conscience, void of any offence. "How much more, then, will the blood of Jesus Christ, who through the eternal Spirit offered himself unblemished to God, cleanse our consciences from acts that lead to death, so that we may serve the living God!" (Hebrews 9:14 NIV). Your conscience no longer condemns you and no longer downgrades your self-esteem. Some people are so bothered by their conscience for the things that they have done that it leads them to complete destruction by suicide.

Your conscience bears witness and testifies of good and evil. When there is something in your life that has to be changed, the Holy Spirit convicts you through your conscience. As a believer, your position has changed from condemnation, which leads to hopelessness and destruction, to conviction, which leads to hope and life.

In the final analysis, it is your heart that decides what action you take. Your heart may listen and follow the prompting of your conscience, or it may override it and follow its own desires. A good and perfect conscience is a safeguard that your heart should consult and ultimately abide by its counsel.

By a straightforward stand of conscience Martin Luther changed the course of Christianity forever. In January of 1521, Pope Leo X declared Luther a heretic and expelled him from the church. He was summoned by Charles V to the imperial Diet at Worms to give an account of his writings. During the second hearing of the Diet, Luther said:

> Unless I am convicted by Scriptures and plain reason—I do not accept the authority of popes and councils, for they have contradicted each other—my conscience is captive to the Word of God. I cannot and will not recant, for to go against conscience is neither right nor safe. God help me.

If men and women of the past would have stood firm on their righteous convictions, the world we live in now would be a better one.

One of the decrees and declarations of the Second Vatican Council was the right to freedom of conscience and freedom of religious beliefs. It declared that in matters of religious beliefs, no one should be forced to act contrary to his or her conscience in public or in private, alone or in association with others. The Catholic Church always believed that, but never did the church put it in such clear focus. Needless to say, in practice it was not always respected nor furthered. The Inquisition is a blunt example.

Historically, the Inquisition was a legal court of the Catholic Church (1233) sometimes administered in cooperation with the civil authorities for the investigation and sentencing of persons professing or accused of formal heresy. Abuses were prevalent. The natural rights were often denied and the accused were even tortured. When Martin Luther was 34 years of age, the papal court began an inquisition in Rome in response to Luther's ideas. He was tried in his absence on charges of heresy. Three years later, Rome restarted the inquisition, which led to his excommunication from the Catholic Church in the same year.

The Spanish Inquisition was granted by special authorization from the Vatican to the Catholic sovereigns, King Ferdinand and Queen Isabella in 1476. It was meant to protect the Jewish and the Moorish converts from retaliation of their fellowmen and from relapse, to seek out the lapsed converts and to keep them from forming harmful alliances with heretical groups. The Inquisition was a ruthless tool of both zealots and political self-seekers who did not shy away from cruel and illegal practices. It was a semi-political machine, a mixture of ecclesiastical and state efforts to protect Christian Spain. In 1492, a law was introduced by which Jews had the choice either to become Christians or else be exiled. The Inquisition spilled over to the Spanish missions in the Americas where it became abusive. It continued, with vastly controlled and changed practices, until the early nineteenth century. What a disgrace for the Christian family! God never forces anybody to become a Christian, even if that means that that person will be lost eternally.

A New Creation

"So for anyone **who is in Christ, there is a new creation**: the old order is gone and a new being is there to see" (2 Corinthians 5:17 NJB).

> You cannot have forgotten that all of us, when **we were baptized into Christ Jesus**, were baptized into his death. So by our baptism into his death we were buried with him, so that as Christ was raised from the dead by the Father's glorious power, we too should begin living a new life (Romans 6:3–4 NJB).

"It is not being circumcised or uncircumcised that matters; but what matters **is a new creation**" (Galatians 6:15 NJB). The baptized person is baptized into Christ Jesus; he is in Christ. Therefore, he is a new creation and can start living a new life.

Circumcision of the Heart

"…and **real circumcision is in the heart,** a thing not of the letter but of the spirit" (Romans 2:29 NJB).

> In him you have been circumcised, with a circumcision performed, not by human hand, but **by the complete stripping of your natural self. This is circumcision according to Christ.** You have been buried with him by your baptism; by which, too, you have been raised up with him through your belief in the power of God who raised him from the dead (Colossians 2:11-12 NJB).

The circumcision of the heart performs a complete stripping of your natural self. Therefore it makes your spiritual birth complete—spirit, mind and body.

At baptism we are baptized with water, symbolizing our dying with Christ and our rising with Christ to the newness of life. We receive forgiveness of our sins, the circumcision of the heart, the indwelling of the Holy Spirit, the pledge of a good conscience, and we are baptized into Christ. The end result is a totally new creation.

One must realize that the necessity of water baptism is a normative rather than an absolute necessity. There are exceptions to water baptism. It is possible to be redeemed through 'baptism of blood' martyrdom for Christ. Or through 'baptism of desire' that is a conscious or even an unconscious desire for baptism. Jesus said, "I have a baptism to be baptized with" (Luke 12:50 KJ, as cited in Strong, 1989), when He had already been baptized.

He had come through water and blood, as John wrote, so that he might be baptized with water and glorified with blood. "He it is who came by water and blood, Jesus Christ, not with water alone but with water and blood, and it is the Spirit that bears witness, for the Spirit is Truth" (1 John 5:6.NJB).

"I have come to bring fire to the earth, and how I wish it were blazing already! There is a baptism I must still receive, and what constraint I am under until it is completed!" (Luke 12:49–50 NJB).

Those who, without knowing of Christianity but act under the inspiration of the Holy Spirit, seek God sincerely and strive to fulfill His will are saved even if they have not been baptized. "For since the creation of the world God's invisible qualities—his eternal power and divine nature—have been clearly seen, being understood from what has been made, so that men are without excuse" (Romans 1:20 NIV).

> But the other spoke up and rebuked him. "Have you no fear of God at all?" he said. "You got the same sentence as he did, but in our case we deserved it: we are paying for what we did. But this man has done nothing wrong." Then he said, "Jesus, remember me when you come into your kingdom."
>
> He answered him, "In truth I tell you, today you will be with me in paradise" (Luke 23:40–43 NJB).

Infant Baptism

Infant baptism stands out as a bone of contention among many Protestants. Some claim that infants are incapable of being baptized validly because infants, they say, are unable to be born again due to their physical immaturity and having not yet reached the age of reason. They claim infants and young children are born again automatically but must accept Jesus Christ when they reach the age of reason in order to reach heaven. What does the Bible say about it? "The promise is for you and your children and for all who are far off—for all whom the Lord our God will call" (Acts 2:39 NIV). This command is universal, not restricted to adults only. The term children includes infants. If we prevent infants from being baptized, we are making a statement that they are unable to have spiritual life, which is nonsense. Jesus set a precedent, as found in Luke 18:15–17:

> People even brought babies to him, for him to touch them; but when the disciples saw this they scolded them. But Jesus called the children to him and said, "Let the little children come to me, and do not stop them; for it is to such as these that the kingdom of God belongs. In truth I tell you, anyone who does not welcome the kingdom of God like a little child will never enter it" (NJB).

Those opposing infant baptism, on grounds that infants are incapable of having faith and since faith is required to be baptized, should carefully consider the following. The Lord did not require infants or young children to make a conscious decision for him; the Godparents or the parents stand for them. As the faith of others can heal a person, so the faith of others can bring life in baptism for their child. The cure of the paralytic man in Luke 5:17–26 shows us how the faith of others was instrumental in getting the man healed.

"After she [Lydia] and her household had been baptized she kept urging us" (Acts 16:15 NJB).

"Late as it was, he took them to wash their wounds, and was baptized then and there with all his household." (Acts 16:33 NJB).

"Yes, I did baptize the family of Stephanas, too" (1 Corinthians 1:16 NJB). There must have been babies in those families, at least in some of them if not in all of them. The Catholic Church always taught infant baptism and baptized babies. It follows apostolic tradition, tradition of the apostles inspired by the Holy Spirit. Apostolic tradition has nothing in common with human tradition that makes the Word of God ineffective. The Early Church did not have the New Testament so they had to rely on apostolic tradition.

Baptism is the circumcision of the heart. In fact baptism has replaced circumcision of the flesh. It too required faith for the adults but not for infants of believers. "In him you have been circumcised, with a circumcision performed, not by human hand, but by the complete stripping of your natural self. This is circumcision according to Christ" (Colossians 2:11 NJB). In Old Testament times, if a man wanted to become a Jew, he had to believe in the God of Israel and be circumcised. In the New Testament, if one wants to become a Christian, one must believe in God and Jesus and be baptized. In the Old Testament, those born of Jewish households could be circumcised in anticipation of the Jewish faith in which they would be raised. Thus, in the New Testament, those born in Christian households can be baptized in anticipation of the Christian faith in which they will be raised.

Many Protestants who object to infant baptism dedicate their children to God as a substitute to baptism. For more information refer to 'dedication of infants'.

The Catholic Church recognizes as valid baptism a baptism by immersion, lowering of the body into the water; by aspersion, the sprinkling of the body with water; and by infusion, the pouring of water over the body. Catholics also recognize as valid baptisms performed by non-Catholics. Anyone may baptize an infant in danger of death; even an aborted fetus should be baptized. If no sign of life is present, then the fetus should be baptized conditionally. Baptism is conferred conditionally when there is doubt concerning a previous baptism or the disposition of the person to be baptized. Through baptism one becomes a member of the body of Christ.

Adult Baptism

Anabaptists, such as the Baptists, the Mennonites, the Hutterites etc., do not recognize infant baptism. That doctrine stems from a violent past. Luther, Calvin and Zwingli considered the position of the Anabaptists heresy. Their main tenet was that baptism is for adults only, making infant baptism invalid. The term 'Anabaptist' (re-baptizer) was pinned on them by their adversaries. It all started in the sixteenth century. In Zurich's City State, as in the rest of the Christian World, every newborn child was baptized. City Council decreed (January 17, 1525) to have all babies baptized within eight days of birth, or the parents would face banishment from the territory. The Anabaptists would not baptize the babies and would re-baptize the adults who were already baptized as babies. On March 17, 1526, the Zurich Council lost patience and decided if they found anyone re-baptizing they would be put to death by drowning. Their reasoning was if the heretics want water let them have it. So, many fled to Germany and Austria. It was like jumping from the frying pan into the fire. In 1529, the Imperial Diet of Spyer proclaimed Anabaptism a heresy, and every court in Christendom was obliged to condemn the heretics to death. Luther joined forces with the Catholics, and they persecuted the Anabaptists intensely. Among the early Anabaptist's missionaries to Tyrol was George Blaurock, a former Catholic priest. He was burned at the stake on September 6, 1529. So was Michael Sattler, a former Benedictine monk, burnt at the stake in Rottenburg-am-Neckar in 1527. Many thousand Anabaptists were executed during the Reformation by fire, by sword but mostly by water. Society is a lot more tolerant nowadays, and Anabaptism is still very much practiced in Protestant circles.

Salvation

Just mention the word 'salvation' and a heated debate among the many Christian factions kicks in. One is born of God by believing in Jesus Christ and by baptism. But to be truly saved, one's cooperation with God during one's lifetime is necessary. Salvation is a matter between God and the individual.

The Age of Reformation was marked by debate among Christians about the ways of salvation. The Catholics settled it almost two thousand years ago, whereas Protestant denominations adopt their own ways. The logical place to become a Christian is the local Church, but for many Protestant churches that's not the case. The Protestant Reformation declared that no church should come between the soul and its maker. John Wycliffe (1320–1384), the English reformer, concluded that the church is a unity that knows nothing of papal primacies and hierarchies, and of the 'sects' of monks, friars, and priests; nor can the salvation of the elect be conditioned by masses, indulgences, penance, or other devices of priestcraft.

The revivalists in New England (1741) believed that it was contrary to the Word of God to permit the unconverted to enter the church building. In the twentieth century, many Christians declared falsely that only members of the Catholic Church could obtain salvation. That heresy stemmed from the errors of the Jacobites in 1442. The Catholic Church never endorsed that heresy but denounced it vehemently.

The local church, be it Protestant or Catholic, is and remains the place *par excellence* to become a Christian and to be brought to maturity in the Christian walk. However, for those who knowingly and deliberately (that is not out of innocent ignorance) commit the sins of heresy (rejecting divinely revealed doctrine) or schism (separating from the Protestant or Catholic Church and or joining a schismatic church) no salvation would be possible until they repented and returned to live in Christian unity.

The Protestant Reformers—Luther, Calvin and Zwingli—stressed salvation by grace alone, whereas the Council of Trent (Catholic) emphasized salvation by grace and human cooperation with God. According to Protestant belief the Christians are justified by faith alone. Here is what the Bible has to say:

> You see that a person is justified by what he does and not by faith alone. In the same way, was not even Rahab the prostitute considered righteous for what she did when she gave lodging to the spies and sent them off in a different direction? As the body without the spirit is dead, so faith without deeds (works) is dead (James 2:24–26 NJB).

"The only thing that counts is faith expressing itself through love" (Galatians 5:6 NIV).

"For we are God's workmanship, created in Christ Jesus to do good works, which God purposed in advance for us to do" (Ephesians 2:10 NJB).

"...continue to work out your salvation with fear and trembling, for it is God who works in you to will and to act according to his good purpose" (Philippians 2:12 NIV).

"In the same way, let your light shine before men, that they may see your good deeds and praise your Father in heaven" (Matthew 5:16 NIV).

What are the works we are talking about? There are works of the flesh and works of love, works of the spirit. Luther gives us a good example of works of the flesh. "I kept the rule so strictly," he recalled years later, "that I may say that if ever a monk got to heaven by his sheer monkery, it was I" (Shelby, 1995, p. 238). Luther sometimes fasted for many days and slept without blankets in freezing winter temperatures. Those are works of the flesh profiting nobody. We will be judged at the end of our lives by the works we did or did not do, works of love.

> Then the righteous will answer him, 'Lord, when did we see you hungry and feed you, or thirsty and give you something to drink? When did we see you a stranger and invite you in, or needing clothes and clothe you? When did we see you sick or in prison and go to visit you?'
> "The king will reply, 'I tell you the truth, whatever you did for one of the least of these brothers of mine, you did for me' (Matthew 25:37–40 NIV).

You may wish to read the whole paragraph, verses 31 to 46.

Only works done while being in Christ and Christ in you are works of love that profit salvation.

Loss of Salvation

The call of a Christian is not a call of passivity, a call to wait and see, a call to lay back, but a call to go forward, to evangelize your surrounding, a call of constant, fervent zeal in fulfilling God's will in your life, a call to bring about God's kingdom on earth. We are created in Christ Jesus to do good works.

"...but anyone who stands firm to the end will be saved" (Matthew 24:13 NJB). Everybody has talents, natural and spiritual talents. Those talents ought to be used to bring about God's kingdom here on earth. We will be judged according to what we did with our talents. We read in the Bible, in the parable of the talents, that the one who received one talent buried it and did nothing with it. It was taken from him. "And throw that worthless servant outside, into the darkness, where there will be weeping and gnashing of teeth!" (Matthew 25:30 NIV). It is a picture of eternal damnation. It does not sound like salvation.

"Remember God's severity as well as his goodness: his severity to those who fell, and his goodness to you as long as you persevere in it; if not, you too will be cut off" (Romans 11:22 NJB). Persevere in God's goodness, as you love Him and your fellow men.

> ...and you may be sure that anyone who tramples on the Son of God, and who treats *the blood of the covenant* which sanctified him as

if it were not holy, and who insults the Spirit of grace, will be condemned to a far severer punishment (Hebrews 10:29 NJB).

"Do not be afraid of those who kill the body but cannot kill the soul; fear him rather who can destroy both body and soul in hell" (Matthew 10:28–29 NJB). Soul stands for your spiritual, your supernatural nature. Salvation can be lost by the choices you make, by your reaction to influence.

"..and anyone who has escaped the pollution of the world by coming to know our Lord and Savior Jesus Christ, and who then allows himself to be entangled and mastered by it a second time, ends up by being worse than he was before" (2 Peter 2:20 NJB).

> "How much more can we be sure, therefore, that, now we have been justified by his death, we shall be saved through him from the retribution of God. For if, while we were enemies, we were reconciled to God through the death of his Son, how much more can we be sure that, being now reconciled, we shall be saved by his life" (Romans 5:9–10 NJB).

> Many will say to me on that day, "Lord, Lord, did we not prophesy in your name, and in your name drive out demons and perform many miracles?" Then I will tell them plainly, "I never knew you. Away from me, you evildoers!" (Matthew 7:22–23 NIV).

"I know your deeds, that you are neither cold nor hot. I wish you were either one or the other! So, because you are lukewarm—neither hot nor cold—I am about to spit you out of my mouth" (Revelation 3:15–16 NIV).

How you live and end your earthly life, the choices you made, the work you did or did not do, all determine your final salvation.

> "To God we are the fragrance of Christ, both among those who are being saved and among those who are on the way to destruction; for these last, the smell of death leading to death, but for the first, the smell of life leading to life" (2 Corinthians 2:15–16 NIV).

9. Christianity: Success or Failure?

Christianity is the responsibility of God. The Holy Spirit is totally in charge, and therefore it cannot fail. We, as individuals, are as successful as the measure in which we rely on the teaching, guidance and help of the Holy Spirit. God delights in using the foolish things of the world and the most unlikely individuals to do His work here on earth. We, as the sons and daughters of God, may lose a battle here and there, but we will never lose the war. Even the lost battles are part of the overall victory, and the victory is ours regardless of what it looks like. Yes Christianity is a great success and not a failure and as long as there are people willing to die to themselves for the kingdom's sake, that victory is assured. Christianity has a built-in insurance for victory and success. There is no other belief system, business or organization whose members are persecuted and put to death that generates a greater success and a greater victory than Christianity.

"I tell you the truth, unless a kernel of wheat falls to the ground and dies, it remains only a single seed. But if it dies, it produces many seeds" (John 12:24 NIV).

Many Christians are looking to return to Acts. In fact, we ought to look forward not backwards. The time of Acts was the beginning, and we now live in the end times. Greater things are in store for us than what the Early Church experienced. Many denominations regressed over the centuries; they are not even close to the early beginnings. Science and technology are far advanced. There is no reason to go back to the Stone Age. Christianity regressed, stayed stagnant and few progressed. It is high time to get in line with the Holy Spirit and to catch up. The key is obedience, obedience to the Word of God and a call to holiness like never before.

Every Christian is called into full-time ministry. There is no vacation in God's kingdom. Christians never cease to be sons and daughters of God. Should we be all pastors, evangelists, teachers, or prophets? Of course not. They are the five-fold ministry to equip the rest: the majority, the workhorse, and the foot soldiers. It is they who ought to do the bulk of God's work. Who are they? They are the housewives, the husbands, the children, the mothers, the fathers, the grandfathers, the grandmothers, the young, the middle aged, the old, in fact everybody. Your mission field is the environment where you live: your family, your work place, your sports arena, your leisure-time place, your church, and your school, college or university. God calls each and every one of you to your place of influence, the place where you are king. There is no retirement, so you will not get bored. From the time you arise in the morning until the time you go to rest, you can be a good influence to someone to bring the kingdom of God closer to that person or you can be a bad influence to someone to distance that person from the kingdom of God. It is your choice. Live in the present and waste no moment; use it for the kingdom of God. Operate in Phase One, and Phase Two: is everybody's mission field.

Become a full-time minister of God's love and mercy. As long as you breathe, there is a calling for your life. Let rivers of living waters gush out from your spirit to give life to anyone who comes in contact with you. You may be lying on a hospital bed or be in jail or any other place; that mandate still applies to you, yes to you. As a Christian, you are the light of the world. When everybody fulfills his calling, God's glory will fill this earth and the King of kings and the Lord of lords will come.

Appendix A

Mind Basics

The encyclopedias and dictionaries are as confused and double minded as most people are, when it comes to defining spirit, mind and soul. It probably originates from the fact that none of them can be seen with the naked eye. The meanings of 'spirit' and 'soul' are interchangeable, and 'soul' and 'mind' as well. The word 'soul' seems to be the culprit, because 'soul' can stand for 'spirit' as well as for 'mind' in addition to ten other meanings.

According to the Gage Canadian dictionary soul has the following meanings (items one to nine only):

1. the spiritual part of a person [the spirit for the believer, the mind for the unbeliever].

2. energy of mind or feeling i.e. She puts her whole soul into her work.

3. a cause of inspiration and energy i.e. She was the soul of the movement to reform nursing.

4. essential part i.e. Brevity is the soul of wit.

5. a person i.e. Don't tell a soul.

6. an embodiment i.e. He is the soul of honor.

7. the spirit of a dead person.

8. among North American blacks, a consciousness of and sense of pride in their African heritage.

9. having to do with or reflecting the cultural heritage of American blacks i.e. Soul food, soul music.

10. life in the physical body: "...and lose his own soul..." (Mark 8:36 NJB).

Soul is a bad word in the sense that it creates confusion and misunderstanding in the mind of most people as opposed to giving a clear, unambiguous picture of what is being said. The more meanings we attach to the word soul, the more confusion we create. I personally use spirit for spirit and mind for mind. The mind comprises your thoughts, memory, imagination, your emotions and your will. Unbelievers think that they have a soul and a body, but believers know that they are a spirit with a mind and a body.

Mind is the unconscious and conscious faculty that perceives, conceives, comprehends, evaluates and reasons, the cognitive and intellectual faculty or state, the emotional faculty or state, and the volitional faculty or state.

The cognitive faculty or state comprehends your thinking, your imagination and your memory.
Thinking is to form or conceive mentally as a thought; to create intellectually as an idea or concept.

Imagination is the act of imagining, or of forming mental images or concepts of what is not actually present to the senses.

Memory is the mental capacity or faculty of retaining and reviewing impressions or of recalling previous experiences.

Emotion is an affective state of consciousness in which joy, sorrow, fear, hate or the like is experienced.

Will is the faculty or power of conscious and especially of deliberate action.

When a person is born again and becomes a Christian, meaning becoming a Christ-like person, the spirit of that person becomes alive. It is a new creation. That person's mind and body are recreated as well, but they need to be transformed, and it will take time and effort. They have to shed their old ways of thinking and of doing.

"Do not conform any longer to the pattern of this world, but be transformed by the renewing of your mind" (Romans 12:2 NIV). Transformed means ceasing to be one thing and becoming another thing. You will have to be spiritually minded; you must act, think and feel according to God's Word. Your mind controls your life. It is your mind that has to be transformed: your thinking, your imagination, your memory, your emotions and your will.

The conscious, subconscious and unconscious all have to be transformed. It is a process, and it will take time and effort.

Conscious: inwardly sensible; aware of one's own existence, emotions, and thoughts or of external objects and conditions.

Subconscious: existing or operating beneath or beyond consciousness, not wholly conscious.

Unconscious: a general name for the mental processes that are not conscious.

Our mind operates in these three distinct zones: the conscious, the subconscious and the unconscious. The subconscious is the bridge between the unconscious and the conscious. Different physical areas of the brain are allotted for the three zones. The key to success in your life depends on your mind. It is in your mind where the battles of your life are taking place. Your mind is the link between your spirit and your body.

Ideal situation

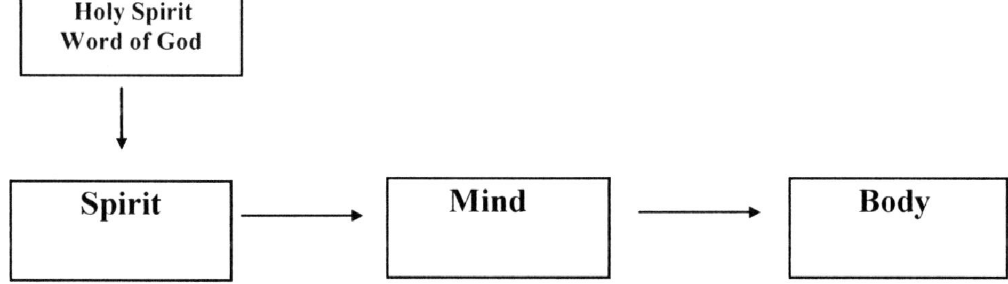

In the ideal situation, the mind is in perfect control, aided by the spirit, knowing the truth and walking in it. In fact, the spirit is the higher authority, but the mind is the administrator.

Bad situation

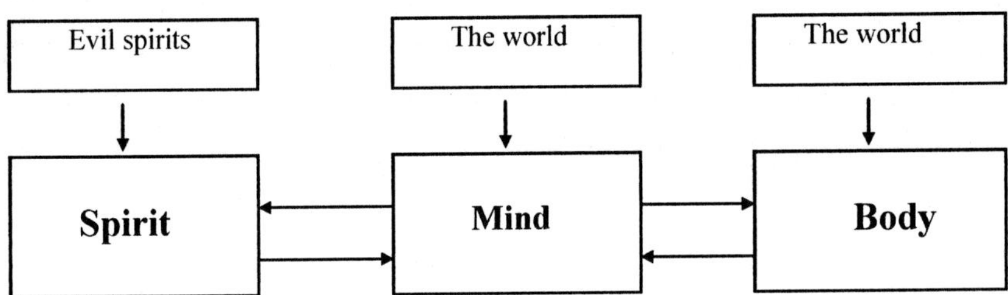

In the bad situation, the mind is controlled by the body and influenced by evil spirits and the world. Deception, destruction and even death may be the result. The spirit lacks the guidance of the Holy Spirit and the knowledge of the Word of God. The mind is thinking the wrong thoughts; it has a defiled imagination and a polluted memory; the emotions are perverted and the will acts irrationally. There is no truth in such a person. Your mind is what decides life and death in your life. Your mind decides if you are successful or not, it is your mind that decides if you will be living a marriage worth living. In this situation the body is the boss.

Controlled situation

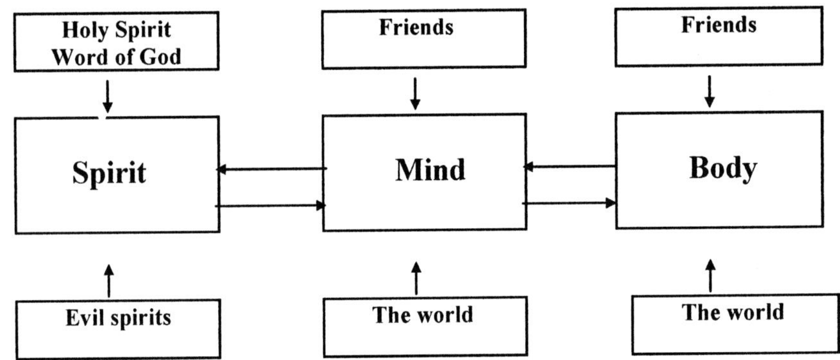

You have three enemies: yourself, the world and evil spirits.

The world in this context means any negative power or influence, untruthfulness originating from persons other than you or from yourself.

Friends means any positive power or influence, truthfulness originating from persons other than you or from yourself.

Evil spirits are the demons, fallen angels and Satan.

There is triple input, good or bad, from your body, your spirit and your mind. Your mind processes that input, good or bad, and acts upon it. Your output depends on your mind. Your input may be all bad, but your output may still be all good. Your mind makes choices, constantly, good or bad. What makes a person great is not the circumstances that person is in but the way that person reacts to those circumstances: his or her choices. We are all accountable for our choices.

Influence as a Vital Force

When a person learns and puts into practice how to handle anything and everything that comes his or her way he or she has it made, no matter what life dishes up. Influence is everything that we perceive with our spiritual and natural senses. Every influence can be a vital force and not a destructive force. We can benefit from everything that influences our lives, the good things as well as the bad things. Nothing should be wasted. Everything should and can make us a better person.

"We are well aware that God works with those who love him, those who have been called in accordance with his purpose, and turns everything to their good" (Romans 8:28 NJB).

Here is God's command, "Love the Lord your God with all your heart and with all your soul and with all your mind and with all your strength" (Mark 12:30 NIV). To be able to do that, there must be unity among spirit, mind (three zones: conscious, subconscious and unconscious) and body. As long as the three zones (spirit, mind and body) are separated, the vital force will instinctively look for the enjoyment of sensation (what is sensed by our senses) and the satisfaction of this enjoyment becomes its goal. The sensation will be captivating and self-centered. The realization of love for instance will be egoistic and negative. The vital force must be assumed by the mind to give it a supernatural dimension. Conjugal love, for example, must be lived by all three zones in unity; peace and joy will be the result.

Any influences such as emotions, words spoken to you, events, sickness and disease, sufferings, good and bad things etc., are forces at your fingertips. They may be positive or negative forces, but it is up to you what the final outcome will be. Criticism either gives life or destruction to you. If you know how to handle it, you may thrive on it.

The force triggered by a positive influence such as love or by a negative influence such as suffering, when put into motion, is inevitably going ahead to its realization, either through a negative, instinctive realization: blockage (inhibition, explosion or compensation) or through a positive, controlled realization: assumption of the desire associated with that influence, desire being realized or not. The desire contains the vital or the destructive force.

Our mind becomes master of the force initiated by a sensible vibration. The mind can take that force, transfer it and use it for a different purpose to that initially intended. It can make us better or bitter, it's your choice. Instead of blocking a sensation, our mind can receive that sensation and use it for another purpose contrary to its original desire. On the other hand, if the mind refuses to receive that sensation and blocks it, our imagination will take hold of it and absorb that force and use it for its own purpose. The imagination can absorb the force instinctively and uncontrollably, or the mind can use it consciously, then it becomes a creative function.

The imagination can revive and put into motion an old sensation without any exterior stimulant or by imagining new situations that can generate new sensations putting into motion new forces, vital or destructive, without exterior stimulation.

Our memory registers all events, similar to videotape, retrievable at will at any time. When your thoughts and the reality of your life join together, when there is a bridge between your thinking and living, between intention and sensation, between intention and act, unity will have been realized.
The first rule for control of the mind is to learn how to receive reality and influence, to receive reality no matter what you feel and to realize what you want realized. What is meant by realization? It means the end result, a concrete achievement that was started by an influence, a good or a bad influence. A bad influence could be a spoken phrase from someone, which offended the hearer. Instead of punching that person out, a bad realization, the hearer channels the force from that influence to a nobler end by assuming it and offering it up to God. It is turned into love, a positive realization, a good result. It will make the hearer a better person; it will build character. Reception is a conscious and voluntary attitude. To accept is in itself an act of consent, agreement and endorsement; it implies your will. To receive signifies receiving without necessarily totally agreeing to what is being received. To receive reality that exists does not mean to consent to what is or to adhere to it. It does not insinuate to give in to it, by weakness, either. On the contrary, to receive reality

demands courage and sometimes heroism, and it suggests the desire and the volition of truth. To receive is to allow silence, which permits one to listen, to hear, to see, to translate before speaking, before making a decision and before acting.

The first reception to achieve is the one of our conscious mind vis-à-vis our personal sensitivity, to be able to remain in control of ourselves and to become available to others. In receiving, you open the door, you let the other person enter and take that person seriously. Too often, we think, speak and act what we feel and not what is real. For example, if someone tells me of an injustice, aggression starts rising within me, which is a normal reaction. To be able to remain in control of the situation, I must receive that aggression caused by the unjust statement. Using that reality as a starting point, I can either receive that aggressive sensation or deny it. Negation will instinctively, automatically set into motion a whole series of actions that will block that deep force, or I can respond 'eye for an eye and tooth for a tooth' and be really aggressive. Your mind must be constantly in a state of openness, availability, a state of reception in regard to everything that may happen to you. If your mind does not take that position of receptivity, your mind will close itself spontaneously and involuntarily and set itself unconsciously and inevitably, to a certain, degree against you.

There are a few false receptions you should be aware of, namely projection, introspection and distraction by your imagination.

Projection is the process of unwittingly ascribing your own attitudes, feelings or the like to others, often as an unconscious defense against a sense of inadequacy or guilt. That person imposes himself or herself on others. We must realize not everybody is like us, and we are not to judge anybody.

Introspection is to look within you, to seal yourself off from your surrounding.

Distraction by your own imagination in facing reality, fooling yourself and making yourself believe things that are not real.

The first thing you should do when you encounter difficulties is to 'stay home' and listen to what is going on, so you will be able to pinpoint the initial cause of your difficulties. Every aggressive manifestation (eye for an eye, tooth for a tooth behavior, silent treatment, *arriere pensees*, smiles that speak volumes) is the proof that you have not assumed your personal sensitive vibration, and you are not in a state of reception to others. You will automatically block others out even if you do not want to. Your state of 'against' will be sensed by others even though no word is spoken. There are people, no matter what happens to them, no matter what is said to them, that cannot be shaken in their foundation. They radiate a serenity, an inner peace that most people find impossible to reach.

Your conscious mind must receive everything, good or bad, joy or suffering. It is the duty of the conscious mind to sort out and to sift what is to be accepted, what you want, can and must realize. Your mind must receive everything but should only accept what is good, or in view of something good. You must receive yourself, the way you are, your temperament, your heredity, your social milieu, your nationality, your failures past and present, your known and unknown desires, your joys and successes, your sufferings, your sensitivity, your gender, your sexuality, your marriage, all events and the list goes on.

Your mind must accept yourself and others. You must accept to learn to love God and all men (men and women), your spouse, your children and everything that is in line with God's Word, everything that is good and pleasing to God.

Learn to Think

Desire is a force capable of becoming a reality. It is a profound force of a temperamental tendency put into motion by an exterior or interior stimulant. Desire finds itself tinted with emotions. Life becomes real through our desires. It is possible to change our wants but impossible to change our desires. Only God can. We are only responsible for the consent to those desires and the direction of those forces. The desires are birthed in our physical body, in our emotions, in our imagination or in our memory. We have a multitude of desires known and unknown. Many of the desires we are unaware of and often we do not want them because of social, moral or personal restrictions. We unconsciously silence them. These are all forces that are mostly realized through compensation, preventing the development of our personality.

Desires are realized on the human level in a negative and captivating way or assumed by the conscious mind aided by our spirit. When that happens, a total unification between spirit, mind and body takes place. Desires that are neither realized nor assumed are blocked automatically, unconsciously leaving in the conscious a force or power that will inevitably look for an outlet or a discharge.

Unity is not achieved, and that force left to itself will act according to the circumstances, the temperament, the past frustrations and so forth. Your mind will have a stubborn will and will block those forces.

A mechanism is a conscious or unconscious mental process that motivates emotional and behavioral responses. It is like a circuit. As long as the conscious mind does not interfere at the opportune moment, the mechanism is set into motion as soon as a similar tonality appears, and it does not matter which point of the circuit is touched, the whole mechanism is set into motion. Words or shocks received trigger connections between the different tendencies of the temperament. The first shock will trigger a series of reactions that will be re-triggered each time with a new shock if it is not assumed. A mechanism can be established consciously or unconsciously, voluntarily or involuntarily.

If you want to change a negative mechanism, you must not try to stop it directly, but impose a positive mechanism that will change little by little the negative mechanism by absorbing all the force and by directing it to its liberation.
Your language has to change. Change "fear to be abandoned," to "abandon the fear."
Change "against" to "for." Here are a few more examples: forbidden to those under sixteen years of age—authorized for those over sixteen years of age; fight against hunger—we unite to give bread to those lacking food.

Build bridges:
- between us, our mind and our deep forces
- between us and God
- between us and the exterior world through words and gestures
- between the conscious and the unconscious through interior conversation.

In inhibition the force stays totally deprived of any activity, is passive and inert. Inhibition is a negative or a negation. It is a state of motionlessness, of insensibility, of passivity and of atony. In general, this state comes from an arrested force that falls. Sickness and disease are often a consequence of this state and the unconscious takes refuge where a person cringes.

The explosion is the opposite of the inhibition. A shock will catapult the force into a brutal, choleric, uncontrolled activity and produce all the disorders like vengeance, physical and mental abuse, etc.

The compensation is a re-orientation of a force that was unable to realize itself through its own channel. It borrows another channel using the strongest tendencies of the temperament under its negative forms. If the mind directs the force, it utilizes the conscious mechanism: the voluntary compensation, key words that will permit a wanted realization by unifying all the forces. Voluntary compensation is the one you adopt consciously and voluntarily in view to direct the force with a precise orientation for it to arrive at an assumption. The force can be released without being realized on its own plane. But you must be firm in allowing yourself a limited time frame in doing so. This force is creative; compensation takes place in the cerebral and instinctive zones.

The mind has two positive powers over the vital, instinctive zone through the word. It can translate the sensible vibration or it can initiate mechanisms, messages that make the sensible forces vibrate and direct them to allow a total being—spirit, mind and body—realization.

Learn to Make Choices of Your Actions and Learn to Realize Them with Your Whole Being—Spirit, Mind and Body

Everything we do, day in, day out, is the means to realize our secondary goal: love others, in view of our primary goal: love God. This is the reason why all our minor acts are very valuable, and we must take them seriously.

The assumption is the reception, through our conscious mind, of the vital force and of the sensible plane; it is the transposition and the utilization of the vital force that becomes sensible and emotional on the spiritual plane. It means, instead of letting our vital force live on the instinctive plane only, the mind realizes through assumption its superior goal, its physical, mental and spiritual ideal. The assumption can only take place through the personal choice. If you assume at the moment of shock, the touched force will avoid all the involuntary and unconscious mechanisms. The choice permits the mind to receive the desire that contains the force and then to accept it through the will. This is the route that must always be respected.

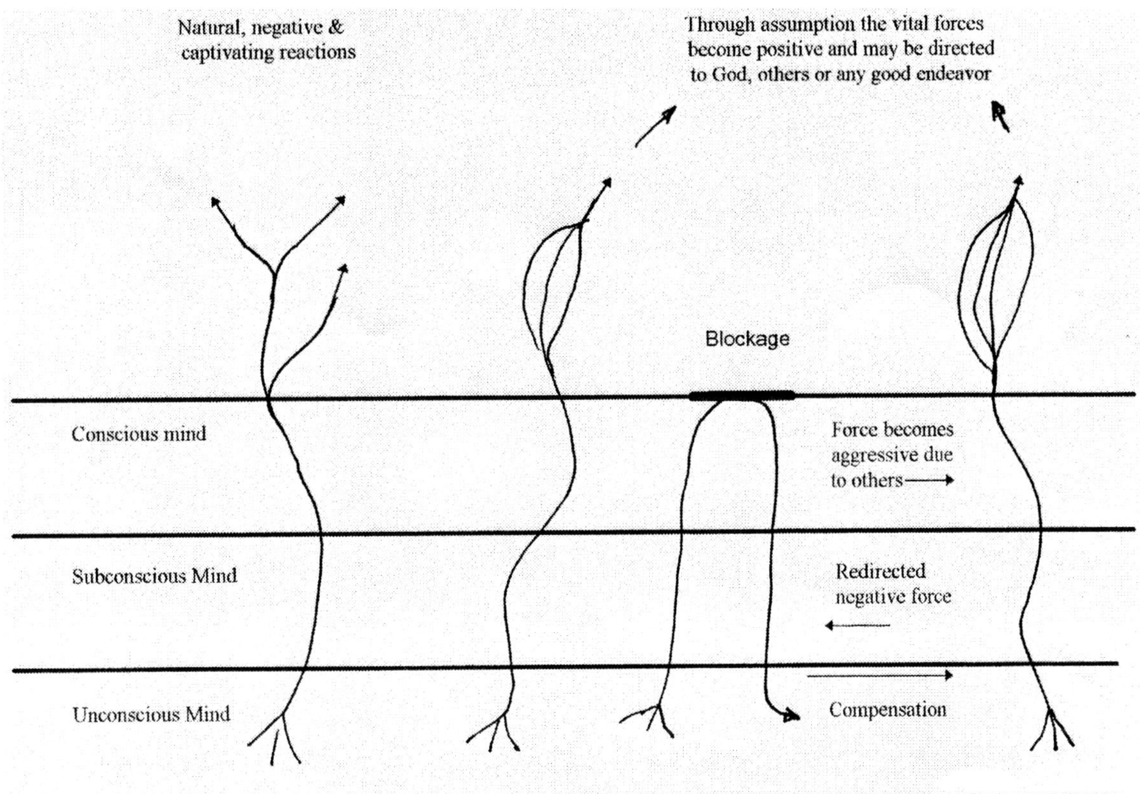

Respective Realizations of a Vital Force

The conscious mind must become aware through the sensations of the nervous system and receive those sensations, registered by the unconscious mind. Those sensations are physical and nervous in nature, while the desire is more mental and touches more on the sensible system.

Through this reception, the mind becomes master of the unconscious force that is put into motion by an exterior or interior stimulant. This force expresses itself by a desire that attracts or repels. If the mind offers to God the vibration and the desire, it directs the force to the spiritual realm or domain.

The assumption of the desire, by taking a stand, results in a purification of the desire. That demands living out the desire as it is at the present moment. It means not living the moment of possession in advance, but in orienting the force of the desire and the painful vibration (not to possess the object of the desire) to God. Your primordial, indispensable attitude must be, "What do I feel?" You must ask yourself this question without thinking anything, so that no reasoning, no supposition and no prohibition intervenes before the word, which translates the sensation, comes to the surface. The role of the conscious mind is to translate and not to impose this word. The force can then be assumed and directed before its realization. The interior discussion realizes the force that cannot be assumed anymore. If this interior discussion takes place, there is nothing that can be done other than assume a failed act.

Here is how to pronounce the words of taking a stand:

#1 I receive the vibration of _____. (Place here the word that surfaced, as it is, e.g. anger, hate, love, etc.)

Receive the sensible vibration that you feel the way it is by letting surface the word that translates it. The force must flow through its real channel; that means it must be assumed by the mind to be able to be directed towards God.

If in certain cases you feel you do not want to assume, it is as though there exists an impossibility to assume. That often reveals there is an unconscious desire of vengeance. There may be a certain fear that once you have assumed, you will not be able anymore to have revenge.

If you become aware of what you feel, without assuming right away, it will be the exterior cause that will be sensed and fixed. This vision will increase the sensible vibration, which quickly becomes intolerable. You must receive the vibration and at the same time direct it towards God. For example, a phrase hurt me. I ask myself the question, "What do I feel?" I listen inwardly, and I hear surface the word "offense". It is through the offering of that offense vibration that I direct my force. The desire is the one of esteem, understanding.

The force of the desire is also realized in the voluntary act because most of the time we do voluntary acts without being aware of the underlying desire and without thinking that it is that desire that possesses the realization force. That desire fights against the voluntary act, and that desire obliges you to make an effort to realize these acts. You offer vibration and desire at the same time.

The suffering, such as unrealized desires, temptations, physical, mental or moral pains—it does not matter what—should neither be treated as negligible nor blocked because it can be a great source of inner wealth. This suffering lived on the sensible plane is the best food for our mind, if we learn to utilize it. We must not repel nor flee from it. Nor should we look for it, but look it straight in the eye, learn to confront it and live it out positively. It will become a means by the voluntary, conscious choice to be taken in view of our ideal. It will permit us to fashion our personality, to be in control.

Joy must and can be utilized to reestablish bridges between body and mind. It can be the normal and privileged bridge of unity between the two when it is able to develop freely and expand with ease. The thought is abstract, but the word spoken is concrete; that is the bond, the tie.

In fact, what you must say is the exact word, the truth in regard to the sensible force to avoid blocking the force, be it yours or somebody else's. But it is very seldom that we say the exact words necessary, so that the sensibility can appease itself. Often we have underlying words that are enough for the mind to understand but not enough for the sensible force to be taken, not having been touched either by the interior nor the exterior word spoken or unspoken. Therefore, it is very important to remember not to look for the cause of the vibration before assuming the felt vibration. To assume the vibration is to receive what is felt as you resent it by recognizing that it is the truth of the sensation without discerning the causes, not even looking for them, not trying to explain them or to condemn them. It is only after the assumption takes place that you may look for the causes if it is necessary to make a decision.

When the force is stretched towards the object of its desire, it is captivating, the tension being a sign of being shackled, chained.

When the desire is assumed and offered up to God, the force relaxes, lets go of its captivating hold and can then be directed to a goal even opposite to its desire because it has become pliable and receptive to the spirit. The assumption of the force in motion can only take place through the exact word.

#2 I direct the force contained in that vibration to Jesus Christ by offering the vibration and the desire of ______. (Name here the one that is underlying, e.g. anger, hate, love, etc.)

Offer to God the sensible vibration through the word that surfaced and at the same time the felt desire.

#3 I choose to do such and such act. Name here those acts that realize the force towards such goals. The underlying desire is always the one that accompanies each vibration.

Make your choice and decide what acts you will initiate with the force of the desire put into motion by the sensible vibration. Remember you cannot carry out an action and its opposite at the same time.

At the moment of your choice, you face a double action to be well executed. First you must let the force of the desire pass to your will, and, secondly, you must keep present to the conscious mind your goal pursued while looking for the means you will employ. By the received and offered desire, the knowledgeable mind will be able to choose the act that will realize the force in motion in the desire. The mind will cease to be the slave of the desire; it will be in control of the force and can receive without fear all felt desires blocking nothing but directing the force towards the anticipated goal. This goal may be the opposite of the desire. More and more, a real freedom will be sensed, interior freedom, first giving way to a freedom vis-à-vis everything that happened in the exterior.

Conclusion

"Be transformed by the renewing of your mind" (Romans 12:2 NIV). The renewing of the mind comes about through the Word of God and the blood of Jesus Christ under the guidance of the Holy Spirit. The absolute truth will be yours. The fiery darts of the evil, you will be able to extinguish. You will demolish arguments and every pretension that sets itself up against the knowledge of God. You will no longer conform to the pattern of the world nor to the evil desires, by taking captive every thought to make it obedient to Christ.

The preceding pages are priceless because they enable you to submit your mind to the Holy Spirit. You can handle any influence coming towards your mind, good or bad, by directing and redirecting them towards your goal: to love God with all your mind.

Your temperament plays an important part of your personality. It mainly resides in your mind, it encroaches on your body and it implicates your spirit. It is part of you and an element of the intrapersonal intelligence.

Appendix B

Purgatory

There is heaven and hell and a third place called prison or paradise. "through whom also he went and preached to the spirits in prison who disobeyed long ago when God waited patiently in the days of Noah while the ark was being built" (1 Peter 3:19–20 NIV).

"Jesus answered him, 'I tell you the truth, today you will be with me in paradise'" (Luke 23:43 NIV). Jesus did not go to heaven the day He died but to prison or paradise. It is a temporary, intermediate state. It is a place where the just who had died before the resurrection of Jesus Christ were waiting for heaven to be opened to them. After His death and before His resurrection, Jesus visited them and preached to them the good news that heaven would now be open to them. These people were not in heaven nor were they experiencing the torments of hell.

The word purgatory is not found in the Bible as such, but that does not prove it does not exist. According to the teaching of the Catholic Church, purgatory will last only until the general judgment. Scriptures declare in Revelations 21:27, "Nothing unclean will enter heaven" (NJB paraphrased). For those who die and died in Christ, the sons of God, purgatory is superfluous.

> If any man builds on this foundation [Christ] using gold, silver, costly stones, wood, hay or straw, his work will be shown for what it is, because the Day will bring it to light. It will be revealed with fire, and the fire will test the quality of each man's work. If what he has built survives, he will receive his reward. If it is burned up, he will suffer loss; he himself will be saved, but only as one escaping through the flames (1 Corinthians 3:12–15 NIV).

The thief on the cross went to paradise because heaven was not yet accessible to anyone. But that changed completely once Jesus rose from death and had conquered death itself. Those who are in Christ and Christ in them are made whole in the twinkling of an eye. We are clothed with the righteousness of Christ; therefore, no purging is required from us. Scriptures tell us to put on Christ. In the parable of the wedding banquet, one man did not put on wedding clothes. He was cast out into darkness (hell) for not having put on Christ.

Prayers for the Departed

Prayers for the dead were practiced by the Jews of the time of the Maccabees, but have even been retained by the Orthodox Jews today, who recite a prayer known as the Mourner's Kaddif for eleven months after the death of a loved one, so that the loved one may be purified.

"For had he not expected the fallen to rise again, it would have been superfluous and foolish to pray for the dead…. Hence, he had this expiatory sacrifice offered for the dead, so that they might be released from their sin" (2 Maccabees 12:44–45 NJB).

The Protestants cut out the books of the Maccabees from the Scriptures in order to avoid accepting this doctrine. Praying and interceding for the departed has value in that God knows everything. Through those prayers and intercessions, God may apply retroactively the grace and understanding to accept Jesus as their savior and redeemer in the last moments of their earthly lives.

Intercession of the Saints

The Apostle's creed declares the spiritual union that exists between the saints in heaven (triumphant church) and the faithful living on earth (militant church). The union between these two groups, the triumphant and the militant believers is called communion of the saints. It is a union of grace and good works and, in recognition of this, the faithful imitate, venerate or honor and pray for the intercession of the saints in heaven. The body of Christ comprises the militant church, which is made up of the living members who actively work out their salvation within faith, love and hope and the triumphant church, which are the saints in heaven. Obviously, the triumphant or glorious church is much more powerful and needs no help whatsoever but can give help to the militant church and its members. We are one body; if one hurts all hurt.

My uncle escaped from the German soldiers on Christmas day in 1944. It meant he had to run across fields into the darkness of a dense forest. He kept running when all of a sudden his departed mother appeared to him and commanded him not to go any further. Exhausted he dropped to the ground. When daylight broke, he realized the abyss just feet away from where he lay. Had he gone any further the night before, he would have fallen to his certain death. This was a direct intervention of a departed saint of the glorious church to help a member of the militant church. The help of the glorious church to the militant church speaks volumes. One has only to look into the lives of the canonized saints of the Catholic Church; the miracles are endless.

Most believers find nothing wrong in asking someone to pray for them but find it difficult that a departed saint could be of any help to them. According to Revelation 5:8, those in heaven not only pray with us, they also pray for us. "Each one had a harp and they were holding golden bowls full of incense, which are the prayers of the saints" (NIV).

Angels do the same.
> An angel came and stood at the altar with a golden censor; and he was given much incense to mingle with the prayers of all saints upon the golden altar before the throne; and the smoke of the incense rose with the prayers of the saints from the hand of the angel before God (Revelation 8:3–4 NJB paraphrased).

Jesus is the mediator of the New Covenant; Jesus is the only mediator between man and God. "For there is one God and one mediator between God and men" (1 Timothy 2:5 NIV).

But this does in no way mean that we cannot or should not ask our fellow Christians to pray for us and with us. Particularly we should ask the intercession of those Christians in heaven, who have already had their sanctification completed. "The prayer of a righteous man is powerful and effective" (James 5:16 NIV). Many, especially the Protestants, cut themselves off from the glorious church. They rather struggle unnecessarily when help from heaven is a prayer away.

Saint Worship?

Protestants shy away from praying to the saints; they deny the communion of the saints just to make sure they do not worship the saints. Their belief is that Catholics do worship saints and thus fall into idolatry. Do Catholics worship the saints? Of course they don't.

The word worship has undergone a change in meaning in English. English people refer to their magistrate as "your Worship", the Americans say, "your Honor". That does not mean that the British worship their magistrates as gods. They simply give them the honor appropriate to their office, and not the honor appropriate to God.

In Scriptures, the term worship is also broad in meaning. The early Christians came to use the Greek term *latria* to refer to the honor that is due to God alone and the term *dulia* to refer to the honor that is due to human beings especially those who lived and died in God's friendship, the saints. A special term, *superdulia,* is used to refer to the special honor given to the Virgin Mary. It indicates that the honor due to her as Christ's mother is beyond the *dulia* given to other saints. It is greater in degree, but still of the same kind. The confusion arises when all three *latria, dulia* and *superdulia* are translated by the English word worship. Catholics adore God but honor Virgin Mary and the saints. The Bible commands us to honor, to venerate our parents. "Honor your father and your mother, so that you may live long in the land the Lord your God is giving you" (Exodus 20:12 NIV). If we ought to honor our earthly parents, how much more should we honor our spiritual mother, Virgin Mary? If there is nothing wrong in honoring the living, who still have an opportunity to fall away from God, how much more should we honor those who are gone before us in the friendship of God, His saints.

Appendix C

Homosexuality

Talk about homosexuality, and you have people reacting in the most unconventional ways. Scorned by society, gays and lesbians stood in the shadow for centuries. Our twentieth century's liberality brought them out of the closet and into the limelight. When AIDS came on the scene, and the majority of infected people were homosexuals, they were beaten and bashed and often deprived of their basic human rights as human beings and citizens. That was wrong then and still is today. People of all walks of life have been infected with AIDS since then, so the shame and abuse have somewhat eased a little.

We hear a lot about homosexual rights. The homosexual community does not talk about basic human rights but about the right to be homosexual, to get married with a same sex partner, to have the same benefits as normal couples, from the state and from the church. It is abnormal to be homosexual and those rights should never be granted to them, neither by any state nor by any church.

Jesus Christ died for every one of us regardless of our sexual orientation. He did not come into the world to condemn us but to save us. God the Father sent His only Son Jesus Christ out of love for us all. Homosexuals should not be scorned nor put to shame but loved in the true Christian sense. God does not hate but loves everybody. God hates sin, and every human being should hate sin. Some people think there is no sin and everything that feels good one should do. Others say, "Live by your conscience; you choose; whatever you choose is right." Our conscience is meant to be a safeguard, some kind of last resort and ultimate authority in dealing with our inner self. But, for many, that conscience is weak, polluted and deceived and no longer fulfills the task it is supposed to fulfill. Only if your conscience confirms it with the Holy Spirit, can you rely on it. You must be led, guided and taught by the Holy Spirit on a continual basis, day by day.

What is sin? Sin is a transgression of a natural or spiritual law affecting or harming your body, mind or spirit and/or the body, mind or spirit of other persons. Homosexual activities are sins; it is a transgression of a natural and spiritual law set forth by God Himself. It is unnatural to have sexual relations between two men or two women; it is a sterile undertaking and there can be no fruitfulness whatsoever.

When civil authorities approve of a so called 'marriage' between two parties of the same sex, they show their lack of understanding of what marriage is all about. It is mind boggling to see the same politicians and leaders being deceived and blinded to such a degree that what is wrong becomes right and what is right becomes wrong.

There are times when governments reward people for breaking natural or spiritual laws. Take abortion for instance. Killing of offspring is against natural and spiritual laws and yet blinded government officials provide physicians and funds for women to get it done. If 100 percent of the people say it is all right, that still does not make a wrong right.

Many homosexuals, counselors and even doctors say, "Gays and lesbians are born that way; there is nothing that can be done". That's a lie, a cop-out and a cheap excuse not to do anything or even to try to change. It is similar to parents who think their child's intelligence is solely determined by heredity. So if a child is born a dummy, he or she will always be a dummy. Nothing could be further from the truth. What determines a child's intelligence depends on the first six years of appropriate, specific stimulation to neurologically organize that child's brain. The result will be a very high I.Q.

Animals come into the world with their structures much more organized to function in almost rigid patterns. Their nervous systems are more complete and the patterns of connections directing activity are almost set and unalterable, but fit for early action. Human beings are born with a tremendous part of their nervous mass unpatterned, unconnected, so that people, depending on where they may happen to have been born, can organize their brains to fit the demands of their surroundings. Man's brain can learn to do in many ways what animals can do only in one fixed way. I repeat, no one is born a gay, a lesbian or a heterosexual. The sexual orientation is a learned function for the human species.

Some say, "There is no cure" Cure is a wrong term because homosexuality is not a disease nor a sickness but an acquired result from a learned faulty mode of doing things, actions repeated innumerable times for years on end, which mold the physical, mental and spiritual body. It takes three weeks to form a habit, and it takes three weeks to break a habit. Homosexuality can be changed, it can be reversed and a normal, healthy way of expressing one's sexuality can be learned. Yes, homosexuals can be completely delivered and set free and become heterosexual through and through.

Because homosexuality is a learned function, to reverse it depends entirely on the individual. Some individuals either do not want to change or do not know how to change or do not know that they can be changed. In a free society, where everybody is entitled to their opinion, the populace at large does not necessarily always opt for the truth but rather what the trend is and often the easy way out. Those so-called educated people, who are misinformed, misled and blind to the truth, who ought to be a guiding light for the less educated, come up with same sex parenting as a valid topic for children's books. During their formative years, preschoolers and first-graders are brainwashed to believe "male moms" and "female dads" are normal. Universities, giving courses along those lines, violate their God-given right as a teaching and educational tool for the public at large. Children of all ages are lured to believe a lie, they are deceived and we, as adults, carry the blame.

Reasons That May Cause Someone To Become A Homosexual Rather Than A Heterosexual

#1. Sexuality as such and all its behaviors are learned functions. Nobody is born a homosexual. To be a homosexual is the sum total of all interior and exterior environmental influences. At the onset, nobody wants to be homosexual but is drawn into it because of lack of knowledge and a sincere desire to do something to correct a wrong sexual behavior pattern.

#2. Our sexuality is fashioned right from birth. Parents, or the lack of parents, have a great influence on children's development. The first six years of a child's life are the most significant for that child's development. A loving family environment is the basis of all normal sexual maturity.

#3. Sexual abuse and molestation by a parent, a brother, a sister, a relative, a friend, a teacher or any other person will often have a dramatic effect on the young child and may wreck and destroy that child's sexual development for life.

#4. A wrong, sterile social environment created by our society will promote homosexuality. Children, teenagers, and adults: all are influenced by it. I call it segregation of the sexes: boarding schools for boys only, boarding schools for girls only, the army (all male or all female), the jails and even religious institutions. There are companies that employ only men and others which employ only women.

All those environments leave a trail of homosexual abuse behind. Not only the child and the young adult but even the adult, the teacher, the superior, all are prone more than in any other social setting to become abnormal in their sexual orientation.

#5. Sexual repression. The sexual drive and the propagation of the species are amongst the strongest drives in human beings. False and erroneous education, as well as a stern repression of that drive, in most cases causes a reversal of sexual orientation. The beautiful sex drive is now destructive, centered on self, and to affirm itself looks for expression in the same sex. Parents, teachers and educators bear a tremendous responsibility to teach the truth through words and actions by being themselves models to their pupils. Sex is neither dirty nor sinful but finds it fulfillment in a loving marriage.

#6. Hormonal influences are often unknown and neglected, yet we all depend on the proper hormones, male or female. The adrenal cortex produces both: male and female hormones in both sexes. However, the main production of sex hormones is secreted by the testes in the male and by the ovaries in the female. Small amounts of the sex hormones of the opposite sex are produced by the adrenal cortex in both sexes. Normally, those hormones are not powerful enough to cause masculinization in the female or femininization in the male. About two percent of sex hormones of the opposite sex are present in a normal man or woman.

The adrenal androgen (male sex hormone) is of physiological significance in females, who otherwise lack androgens. It is responsible for androgen-dependent processes in the female, such as growth of pubic and axillary hair, enhancement of the pubertal growth spurt and development and maintenance of the female sex drive. In the male the active intra-cellular androgen is responsible for development of the prostate and bulbourethral glands as well as the seminal vesicles.

Male and female hormones can be out of proportion in either sex, which can lead to a "liking" of a same sex person, and those persons may display the secondary sex characteristics of the opposite sex.

#7. Lack of proper exposure to the opposite sex is very important in early childhood and teenage years. A girl growing up without the father takes on a masculine image and a boy growing up without the father around becomes effeminate; he takes on the character of the mother. If the mother is missing, proper development is also hampered; love's ability is affected.

Hormones affect men and women, not only when taken orally but also through the skin or just by being in close proximity. Men who extracted estrogen from the urine of pregnant mares and those working to produce drugs (estrogen, progesterone, etc..) became impotent and developed breast tissue. Some doctors prescribe patches to supplement extra estrogen for menopausal women. A patch is applied to the skin and the patch releases a small amount of synthetic estrogen in a continuous way. It flows from the patch to the skin to the blood. A male environment is able to influence menses and ovulation in women exposed to that environment, and a female environment will bring about a synchronization in the menstruation habits of the women exposed to that environment like mother and daughter, office workers, etc.. The hormones of a person exercise a regulatory affect on the opposite sex, living in close proximity. A widow, who has lost her male companion, often displays a hormonal imbalance.

For a man to stay sexually healthy, he must be exposed to a female, and for a woman to stay sexually healthy, she must be exposed to a male and for boys and girls to develop properly they must be exposed to both males and females. The family is that ideal environment. Spend some quality time with your wife, your husband and your children.

#8. Spiritual influence. As spiritual beings, we are all influenced either by the Holy Spirit or by evil spirits. Our enemy, an evil spirit or the devil, loves and delights to see human beings get off track, especially in sexual matters, because the destruction can be complete and lasting and often involves more than one person.

> They exchanged the truth of God for a lie, and worshiped and served created things rather than the Creator—who is forever praised. Because of this [worshiping created things rather than God, which is idolatry] God gave them over to shameful lusts. Even their women exchanged natural relations for unnatural ones [lesbians]. In the same way the men also abandoned natural relations with women and were inflamed with lust for one another [gays]. Men committed indecent acts with other men, and received in themselves the due penalty for their perversion (Romans 1:25–27 NIV).

I have mentioned eight reasons why a person may have become a homosexual. Every homosexual is influenced by evil spirits; if that were not the case they would not be homosexual because to be influenced by the Holy Spirit excludes homosexuality. All other reasons are contributing factors only. Any of those factors do not necessarily influence a person to become a homosexual. Most people lack a clear understanding of what causes homosexuality and therefore if they are gay or lesbian they accept the fact; I should say accept the lie, that nothing can be done. If you are sincere, and you want with your whole being to become a normal person in respect to sexual orientation then the next paragraph is for you.

What Can I Do To Become A Normal Heterosexual?

Sexuality as well as homosexuality involves your total being—spirit, mind and body. To be successful you must address all three areas of your human nature.

Spirit

- Have a loving, personal relationship with God the Father, God the Son and God the Holy Spirit. Let the Holy Spirit lead, guide and teach you day by day.
- Feed your spirit with spiritual food, which is the word of God: the Bible.
- Forgive anybody who may have done wrong to you in any area of your life.
- Speak victory and not defeat.
- Ask God to change you, to heal you, to deliver and set you free from the bondage of homosexuality.

Mind

Learn how to control yourself through your mind. Receive everything, including your homosexual desires, but do not accept them; rather redirect them through assumption towards your new goal.

Use visualization as a re-educative tool. If you have a spouse of the opposite sex, he or she can be of great help to you.

Sexual gratification caused by stimulation by the same sex partner, male to male or female to female, will soon become a habit (21 days) and the object of sex, I should say the target person, will in the future be directed exclusively to that same sex partner. Sexual stimulation aided by thoughts, feelings and imagination will translate into acts and actions.

Something is only sexual in the measure it activates the sexual cerebral structure and the awareness or consciousness. If a sexual message or a thought that is homosexual is taken in a different way by the brain, it ceases to be homosexual and no longer has any homosexual power.

Awareness gives us the capacity for judgment, differentiation, generalization, the capacity for abstract thoughts, imagination and so forth. The delay between thought and action is the basis of awareness. Think first, then act.

The delay between a thought process and its translation into action is long enough to make it possible to inhibit it. This possibility of creating the image of an action and then delaying its execution, postponing it or preventing it altogether is the basis of imagination and intellectual judgment.

Learn the beauty of the opposite sex. Look forward to meeting new friends and people of the opposite sex. If you were mistreated or abused by someone of the opposite sex remember there are a lot of good people of both sexes around.

Learn how the brain functions, and choose an appropriate mode of action.

Body

Change your environment, quit your homosexual friends, and let them know you are changing. Sometimes it demands quitting your job, finding a new place to live or moving to another city or town. Start anew.

Whatever you do, make sure you find yourself in a mixed environment, men and women, and positively look out for the beauty in the physiology and psychology of the opposite sex.

See a doctor to find out if your male and female hormones are in the right proportions. The liver converts testosterone and androgen from adrenal source to androsterone and etiocholanolone; both are excreted in the urine. The ratio of androsterone to etiocholanolone can be used to discriminate between heterosexuals and homosexuals. Homosexuals excrete less androsterone than etiocholanolone, while heterosexual males secrete more androsterone than etiocholanolone.

Do a development test on yourself. (Refer to the book "HOW TO AND WHEN" published by SonSet Publishing House) If you fail in any of the levels and stages, do the appropriate exercises regardless of your age, to reprogram your brain.

When we learn a new task, we seldom succeed the first time. A child who learns to walk, falls more than once, but he or she gets up and continues and after a while walks perfectly. So if you do not succeed every day, do not be discouraged but continue diligently, and you will be successful. As a man thinks, so he is, so think highly of yourself no matter what your shortcomings. We all have different talents and I.Q.'s. What is required from us is to work diligently and not to give up. I personally prefer someone who works hard, who has little talent, than someone who works little with a lot of talent.

Remember a single person is not complete, it takes A and B, a man and a woman to be complete. Two A's or two B's by themselves do not make a complete entity and never will make a marriage either. Make the right choice; it is in your power. Your well-being—spirit, mind and body—depend on that choice.

References

The Amplified Bible, Old Testament (1965, 1987). Zondervan Corporation: Grand Rapids, Michigan.

The Amplified, New Testament (1958, 1987) The Lockman Foundation: La Habra, California.

Used by permission.

Bonnke, R. (2003). Correspondence.

Broderick, R.C. (1987). *The Catholic Encyclopedia.* Thomas Nelson Publishers: Nashville, Tennessee.

Catholic Catechism, (1997) Libreria Editrice Vaticana: Citta del Vaticano.

Gage Canadian Dictionary (1984). Gage Publishing Limited: Toronto.

Grun, G. (1997). *How To And When.* SonSet Publishing House: Richmond, B.C.

The Holy Bible, New International Version ®. NIV ®. (1973, 1978, 1984). Zondervan Publishing House: Grand Rapids, Michigan. Used by permission of Zondervan Publishing House. All rights reserved.

King James Bible, 1890.

Luther, M. (1524) *Large Catechism.* In Bente F., & Dan, W.H.T. (Trans.). (1921) *Triglot Concordia: The Symbolical Books of the Evangelical Lutheran Church.* Concordia Publishing House: St. Louis.

Nelson's Illustrated Bible Dictionary. (1986). Thomas Nelson Publishers: Nashville, Tennessee

The New Jerusalem Bible. (1997). Doubleday, Dell Publishing Group Inc.: New York, N.Y.

Pope John Paul II. (1995). *Evangelium Vitae* (encyclical). The Vatican: Vatican City.

Shelby, B.L. (1995). *Church History In Plain Language.* Word Publishing: Dallas, Texas.

Stravinskas, P. *OSVs Catholic Encyclopedia Revised*-CD-Rom 1997

Strong, J., S.T.D., LL.DD. (1890, 1989). *Strong's Exhaustive Concordance of the Bible* (45th printing). World Bible Publishers Inc.: Iowa Falls, Iowa.

12 Heresies of Christianity (2003) *The Heresy of Luther: Reformation Undone.* Abstract retrieved from Sullivan-County database Aug. 2005 (http://www.sullivan-county.com/id3/luther1.htm)

Walsh, M. (1984). *The Popes.* Bonanza Books: New York, N.Y.

Wikipedia, the free encyclopedia. http://en.wikipedia.org/wiki/Pope John II.